Crystals *for* Everyday Living

Crystals *for* Everyday Living

Bring happiness to your home, achieve your goals,
and enhance every element of your well-being

Philip Permutt

CICO BOOKS
LONDON NEW YORK

Published in 2024 by CICO Books
An imprint of Ryland Peters & Small Ltd

20–21 Jockey's Fields   341 E 116th St
London WC1R 4BW   New York, NY 10029

www.rylandpeters.com

10 9 8 7 6 5 4 3 2 1

A CIP catalog record for this book is available from
the Library of Congress and the British Library.

ISBN: 978-1-80065-375-7

Printed in China

Publishing manager: Carmel Edmonds
Editor: Kristy Richardson
Senior designer: Emily Breen
Art director: Sally Powell
Creative director: Leslie Harrington
Production manager: Gordana Simakovic
Head of production: Patricia Harrington

SAFETY NOTE
Please note that while the
descriptions of the properties of
crystals refer to healing benefits,
they are not intended to replace
diagnosis of illness or ailments, or
healing or medicine. Always consult
your doctor or other health
professional in the case of illness.

Contents

Introduction 6

Chapter 1
Crystals in Your World 8

Chapter 2
Crystals in Your Home 22

Chapter 3
Crystals at Work 44

Chapter 4
Lifestyle Crystals 68

Chapter 5
The Crystal Finder 94

Further Reading, Resources, and Glossary 137
Index of Crystals 140
Index 142
Acknowledgments and Picture Credits 144

Introduction

This book grew from an idea. It all just started as a thought: if you do anything with conscious intent, it amplifies the power and efficacy of whatever it is you are doing. And the whole book flows from this simple understanding. Within these pages you will see how consciously welcoming crystals and their helpful, healing energies into your life will bring happiness to your home, enable you to achieve your goals, and enhance every element of your energy and well-being, easily and effectively. You will feel happier, have more confidence, and be emotionally stronger. Your health will improve, you will become more successful, and you will enjoy all life has to offer.

I came to crystals in 1992 following a serious illness. After severing the sciatic nerve to my right leg in a life-saving operation, the surgeon told me that I wouldn't walk again, so I tried every alternative treatment I could find to heal me. I walked out of the hospital six weeks and two days later. Crystals helped me achieve this and have been with me ever since.

Many people look toward crystal healing as a complimentary healing modality for physical, emotional, mental, and spiritual issues, but crystals can help with so much more, transforming each area of your life with healthy, happy crystal energy.

Crystals are always around me: worn by me, kept by my bed, and placed in my living room, study, and kitchen—in fact, in every room in my house. You will also find them in my garden, my showroom, and my car, accompanying me wherever I travel. They help make life flow better, release daily stress, and even, perhaps, reveal some of the lessons we are on this planet to discover. Everything within the book is real. You will read many examples of my own crystals and how I work with them in a wide range of situations. They become crystal helpers, my assistants in everyday life. They can become yours, too.

Chapter 1

Crystals in Your World

What can crystals do for us? 10

So, what else can crystals do for us? 12

Choosing crystals 14

How quickly do crystals work? 16

Crystals and astrology 18

Crystal care 20

What can crystals do for us?

Crystals are amazing, healing tools. They can lift you up when you're feeling down, heal physical, emotional, mental, or spiritual wounds, and even help you to make decisions along your life path. They are truly magical.

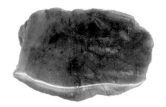

Crystals, such as labradorite, can fill your world with magic.

Magic is defined as something we witness but cannot yet explain … "yet" is the key word here. From the invention of controlled fire to space travel, each jump in technological development has led to wondrous new things for mankind. Each one seemed magical at the time, and each time there have been doubters—those stuck in their old ways, resisting new technology. As science opens new frontiers of possibility and understanding, many of the things which were once called "magic" are now in common usage. They are all around you, every day, packed into what we consider mundane 21st-century living … something our ancestors would have called "magic!"

All innovations in science and technology, such as space travel, once seemed wondrous and "magic."

How old is crystal technology?

Crystals have been at the cutting edge of human technology and possibility since we humans first started walking upright on two legs. The prehistory of human evolution can be witnessed at the Cradle of Humankind, a series of caves north of Johannesburg, Republic of South Africa. Some of the excavations at this UNESCO site take us back to around 3.5 million years go. As each layer of excavation reveals an earlier aeon, from our ancestral prehuman species right the way through to today's *Homo sapiens* (that's you and me), there is one thing each era has in common … crystals.

The earliest humanoid burials date back some 335,000 years. Skeletons, found buried ritually in graves, were discovered by paleoanthropologist Dr Lee Berger in the Rising Star Cave System at the Cradle of Humankind. These are *Homo naledi*, which are perhaps the last pre-*Homo sapiens* species from whom we evolved into today's modern human beings. The ritual markings, carved into smoothed rocks with stone tools, were believed by anthropologists to be linked to belief in an afterlife of some description. Other stone artifacts were also found nearby.

Humans have worked with crystals, such as this Stone Age flint knife, since the dawn of humanity.

In the Kalahari Desert, Republic of South Africa, Dr Jayne Wilkins discovered crystals collected by humans for spiritual use over 105,000 years ago. Described as "non-utilitarian objects" (objects which have been fashioned or placed somewhere for spiritual, beauty, or ornamentation purposes), these calcite crystals were found at a sacred site far from their natural environment. In other words, they were moved there by prehistoric man for a specific and special purpose.

The first humanoid tools were made from chert (often the flint variety of chert), which was made into many things, including scrapers and knives. Chert and pyrite also helped to make sparks for fire. Over the millennia, these tools developed in intricacy and efficiency into axes, spearheads, and arrowheads, and have continued to develop throughout the 21st century into technology for computers, cell phones, lasers, and space travel.

A collection of crystals, such as apatite (left) and spirit quartz (far left), can work together with citrine to treat an underlying cause.

So, what else can crystals do for us?

The question is never "Do crystals work?" or "What can they do for us?" It is always "What can't crystals do!"

Each crystal only does one specific thing. Helping that crystal do that one thing—to be as good as it can be—can affect and change so many things in your life. Citrine, for example, balances the cells in the bowel that absorb nutrients. But it can also aid recovery from injury, maintain a healthy body weight, boost the immune system, and so much more (see box, opposite.)

All crystals affect us in different ways and can often help with many symptoms, but it's in dealing with the cause of a condition that crystals come into their own. For example, if you feel you need to balance your weight, citrine will help if you have a digestive disorder. However, if the cause is emotional, then apatite will work much better for you. If the cause comes from social pressure, then spirit quartz may work better still. In reality, there are often several causes. A bowel disorder such as Crohn's disease can affect weight loss and weight gain, but the condition itself is affected by stress and emotional and social pressure, as well as diet and a genetic predisposition to the condition. In this way, we may need a collection of crystals to help balance all the different aspects of a condition or situation.

The power of citrine

Crystals help your body, mind, emotions, and soul find balance, making you happier and healthier. For example, let's look at citrine, which balances the cells in the bowel that absorb nutrients. Sounds simple. But how does this affect your body, mind, emotions, and spirit?

Well, when we absorb the nutrients we need from whatever food we are eating, we end up with more nutrients flowing around our body. These nutrients make it easier for our bodies to repair quickly, whether from a minor bruise or when recovering from a major operation. So, citrine will help your body to repair itself more quickly.

When you are absorbing the balanced nutrients that you need, it is easier to find and maintain your natural weight. There is no "perfect" weight but a perfect size that is unique to each of us. Everyone is individual and crystals treat us as such. In this way, citrine may be good for weight loss or weight gain.

When there are more nutrients flowing around your body, your heart doesn't need to pump as hard to get nutrients to where they are needed. So citrine is good for your heart health.

Blood flowing more easily around your body moves more oxygen to your brain, which boosts both logical and creative thought. So, citrine is also good for all mental processes, including mental healing.

The blood flowing around your body also carries white blood cells, powerful enforcers of the immune system. These blood cells are like biological bouncers evicting troublemaking bacteria and viruses from your system. So citrine gives you protection against the germs and bugs that are all around us in our environment.

I can go on and on with this example of what citrine can help with, and you may well ask "Well, what can't citrine do?"

The simple, balancing qualities of citrine in one area can affect and improve the body, soul, heart, and mind.

Choosing crystals

The key to choosing crystals is your own intuitive awareness of the crystals you encounter. Start by being aware of the different crystals you are drawn to, be mindful of the ones that repel you, and ignore all the others for the time being.

The crystals you like—the ones that make you feel good or that make you smile—will help you with things you need or want in your life right now. You will often notice quick rewards working with these crystals.

Crystals that you are drawn to will always help you with something you are doing or want to do.

The ones that repel you—that make you feel uneasy, nauseous, or are difficult to even pick up—are the life-changing crystals. They are touching something deep down inside you that you don't want to look at. Even though the process may be uncomfortable at times, the rewards are amazing. When this initial discomfort passes—and it will—life will seem better than it's ever been.

Some crystals just work for almost everyone all the time. Calcite, for example, is always calming and the green variety works magically for anxiety and panic attacks. Others just seem to work in certain circumstances without us really knowing why, such as an elixir of amber to ease constipation. (A crystal elixir is water in which a crystal has been immersed.) Crystals like these are a great place to start for choosing crystals for everyday living, while others will require a little consideration.

EVERYDAY SOLUTIONS

An easy way to choose crystals for everyday living is to look at the common things that can stop us enjoying life every day.

Stress or grief can have a huge impact on daily life and affects everyone differently. Another obvious example is worry—the single, most useless human emotion there is! Once you have thought through, planned, and actioned everything you can about a situation, continuing to think about whether you have done enough, or the right thing, or whatever else is purposeless. Tourmaline is a fabulous crystal to help you with this part. It works in two ways, firstly to help you to focus on the matter in hand and secondly to let go of worry after you have done everything you can. Coincidentally, it's also great for stopping you worrying about what other people think of you, which can free you up to live your life to your fullest potential.

Sometimes our needs are less obvious, or they may be a combination of many different factors. We'll look at these in more detail in Chapter 4 (see page 68.)

Green calcite (top) can help if you suffer from anxiety, and tourmaline (center) eases the symptoms of worry. Amber (bottom) can make an elixir that has healing effects for almost everyone who uses it.

How quickly do crystals work?

Sometimes you have an immediate, almost magical, reaction to a crystal. You buy a new crystal, instantly feel better, and it's as simple as that. However, at other times, it can take longer for you to see the benefits.

Crystals will always start working straightaway and you may feel nothing, start to feel subtle changes, or notice improvement immediately. As a simple guide (but not definitive), the longer the problem has been going on in your life, the longer it will take for crystals to work at their full potential.

For long-term, chronic situations, such as patterns that you have been repeating throughout your life or issues triggered in childhood, crystals may take a while to work. It may take some time while they help you to fully release the associated energy and move on.

Try the exercise opposite to increase your awareness of the crystals that will work for you. With practice, you will soon start to sense your connection with appropriate crystals straightaway.

You will feel the effects of some crystals immediately, while others may take longer to reach their full potential.

Crystal awareness

This exercise will help you to develop your intuition, not just with crystals, but in every aspect of awareness in your life. Before you start, gather your crystals on a table, on the floor, on a tray, or in a bowl. If you have lots of crystals, then you might want to try this exercise with some of them rather than all!

1 Sit or stand in front of your crystals and take three deep breaths into your belly.
2 Close your eyes tightly and count to ten. Feel the tension in your face during these ten seconds.
3 Open your eyes and notice which crystals you see first. Which ones jump out at you? Which ones are waving, sparkly, shiny, or special? Consider how you feel about each of these crystals and how you feel about them as a group.
4 Now repeat steps 1 and 2.
5 Open your eyes, but this time, notice which crystals you don't like the look of. Which ones turn you off, or feel dark, hostile, or unwelcoming? Again, consider how you feel about each of these crystals and how you feel about them as a group.
6 Now, look up the crystals that sparked a strong reaction in The Crystal Finder (see pages 94–136). Do they relate to anything that's going on in your life now or in the past?

Practice crystal awareness to develop your intuition and recognize the crystals that you are naturally drawn to.

Crystals and astrology

There are crystals that tie in with day and night, times of the day, and days of the week. Different cultures throughout history have linked stones to planets, months, seasons, and the zodiac. All of these are good, valid reasons for selecting a crystal.

Astrologers believe that when you are born your body has a natural vibration linked to the Universe of which you are part. If this can be recreated around you all the time, then everything in your life will flow better. Your zodiac (sun) sign is determined by the position of the Sun in relation to the Earth at your time of birth. Dates change slightly because our calendar doesn't exactly match the Earth's orbit round the Sun. If you are born on the cusp, check an ephemeris (see page 137) for exact times and dates.

Carrying or wearing your birthstone replicates the vibrations of the stars and planets at your time of birth. These will be drawn down toward you, boosting your aura. This is protective physically, emotionally, mentally, and spiritually. It is also thought that these birthstones will increase your body's own healing power. You will have more energy, recover quicker from illness and injury, and feel stronger emotionally and mentally to cope with stress.

The birthstones (see box, opposite) shouldn't restrict you in your choice of crystals. If you feel drawn to a specific crystal, it will benefit you even if you don't know how or why you have been drawn to it, and regardless of whether it is your birthstone or not.

There are many different birthstones for each star sign. The chart shown opposite offers a typical, but not definitive, selection.

Capricorns can boost their aura by wearing tiger's eye, one of the birthstones that links to the alignment of the stars and planets at their time of birth.

Typical birthstones

Zodiac signs	Dates	Crystal	
♈ Aries	March 21st–April 20th	Bloodstone	
♉ Taurus	April 21st–May 21st	Jade	
♊ Gemini	May 22nd–June 21st	Agate	
♋ Cancer	June 22nd–July 23rd	Moonstone	
♌ Leo	July 24th–August 23rd	Jasper	
♍ Virgo	August 24th–September 23rd	Carnelian	
♎ Libra	September 24th–October 23rd	Rose quartz	
♏ Scorpio	October 24th–November 22nd	Unakite	
♐ Sagittarius	November 23rd–December 21st	Obsidian	
♓ Capricorn	December 22nd–January 20th	Tiger's eye	
♒ Aquarius	January 21st–February 19th	Quartz	
♑ Pisces	February 20th–March 20th	Amethyst	

Crystal care

Crystals naturally pick up energy. They absorb energy from you, from other people, and from the environments in which they live. Traditional cleansing methods help to release energy buildup that your crystals have absorbed, and which is no longer needed.

Crystals also need physically cleaning as they can become dusty. Dust sticks with an electrostatic charge that affects the electric potential of crystals and also blocks out light, which reduces the quantity of photons a crystal can focus. To remove dust, lightly brush your crystals with a soft brush—a clean makeup brush or small paintbrush is ideal. Do this regularly to avoid dust buildup.

You can also clean your crystals by placing them in a bowl and immersing them in a solution of water and a little mild, good-quality detergent. However, if a crystal carries a "no elixir" warning in The Crystal Finder (see pages 94–136), do not use water-cleansing methods. Afterward, rinse them thoroughly with water to make them sparkle. Leave your crystals to dry naturally or pat them gently with a soft cloth.

Traditional ways to cleanse your crystal

You can see when your crystals need energetically cleansing—they lose their sparkle, brightness, and even color, and may also feel sticky to the touch.

Sound: If you have a lot of crystals, by far the simplest and most effective way of cleansing them is with sound. Tingsha are perfect and can also be used to cleanse your home, workplace, yourself, or others. You can also use drumming, chanting, classical music, loud rock, or drum-and-bass!

Tingsha are perfect for cleansing crystals with sound.

Running water: Hold your crystal under running water for a few minutes (or longer if it's been working hard or hasn't been cleansed for a while).

Incense: Let frankincense, sandalwood, sage, or Palo Santo smoke waft over your crystal. You can also use a smudge stick, which is a bundle of herbs (usually sage) that are burned during cleansing rituals.

Moonlight: Leave your crystal in moonlight, especially the light of a full or new moon.

Earth: Bury your crystal in the earth and leave it there for two weeks. Bury it when the Moon is full and unearth it at the time of a new moon.

Selenite/amethyst/quartz: Place your crystal on a selenite plate or flat crystal, an amethyst bed or quartz cluster, or inside a geode.

Sunlight: Leave your crystal in sunlight. You can also dry your crystals in the sun after washing them. Beware, though—quartz crystals, especially crystal balls, will focus the Sun's rays and can be a fire risk. Take appropriate precautions by not leaving quartz unattended in sunlight for any length of time, and do not place on or near any flammable objects. Please be aware some crystals may fade in sunlight too.

Breath or clear energy: Exposing your crystal to your breath is cleansing. Inhale deeply, focus your intent (for cleansing), and breathe out over the crystal. Any clear energy, such as reiki, can also be used in a similar way.

Crystals can be cleansed of surplus energy with running water (above) or with incense (below).

Chapter 2

Crystals in Your Home

Living with crystals 24

Feng shui 26

A room-by-room exploration 30

Chakras in the home 42

Living with crystals

Crystals are everywhere—in technology, art, or placed with energetic or healing intent. You can channel their energy in different areas around your home to help enhance your everyday life.

Do you recognize new sensations when you bring a crystal home or perhaps visit a friend who has lots and lots of crystals? Simply placing crystals in a room will alter the energetic influences in the space. They transform the energy in their surroundings and bring balance to mind, body, and spirit, as well as the space itself.

You can change the energy in any room whenever you want to focus on a particular feeling, from calm and relaxed, to clear and decisive, or perhaps sensual and sexy. The first—and maybe only—question to ask yourself is what you want from your home and the different areas in it. Which rooms need to feel secure, calm, and peaceful? Which rooms need to be studiously focused, creative, and inspiring? Perhaps you would like to create warm, open, social areas for family and friends, or sensual, cozy rooms and intimate spaces. All these energies making a happy, healthy home for you and your family to live in.

A citrine crystal can bring joy and happiness to any room.

Opposite: Choose crystals for the qualities that you wish to bring to your space, from calming and peaceful to energetic and inspiring.

Feng shui

Feng shui is the flow of *chi*, or life-force energy, through places and structures. It follows the idea that everything is connected in time and space through *chi*. Commonly referred to as "the way of *feng* (wind) and *shui* (water)," it is made in part of yin (passive energy) and part yang (active energy). By changing the energy in a place, you can transform the way you feel, and in turn, how you behave, and even the outcome of events.

Feng shui is a traditional Taoist practice that, originally, provided guidance on the best placement and facing direction for a home or spiritual building, such as a temple or tomb. In both contemporary Western and Chinese culture, feng shui can provide ways to either help balance the available energies in your home or benefit from them.

THE BAGUA MAP

Applying basic feng shui principles to your living space can provide a useful road map to look around your home. The chart shown opposite is called a bagua map, over which you can draw a floor plan of the rooms in your home. You can then use the chart to understand how the different areas of your home may influence certain areas of your life. Each area is linked to a color and crystals. Crystals can bring color that can alter the feeling of a room without having to redecorate, but they also bring an energy all of their own, which enhances the areas of your life represented in the room. On the bagua, I offer a quick guide to crystals to consider for each room to enhance its functionality. The Crystal Finder (see pages 94–136) is also color-coordinated, so you can dive straight in there for more color ideas and lifestyle crystals.

Opposite: Use a bagua to understand how different areas of your home influence certain aspects of your life, and how the energy of each area can be changed with crystals. The crystals pictured are shown in bold.

WEALTH AND PROSPERITY

Ametrine, citrine, tiger's eye

FAME AND REPUTATION

Copper, **carnelian**, vanadinite, amethyst, tourmaline

LOVE AND MARRIAGE

Rose quartz, morganite, emerald, kunzite, pink opal, angel aura quartz

HEALTH AND ANCESTORS

Petrified wood, **malachite**, abalone shell, bowenite

HEALTH AND CENTER

Clear quartz, **golden healer quartz**, hematite

CHILDREN AND CREATIVITY

Blue calcite, dalmatian stone, **snow quartz**, sugilite

KNOWLEDGE AND SELF-CULTIVATION

Jade, **lapis lazuli**, ruby

CAREER AND LIFE PATH

Tourmaline (black), pyrite, obsidian, **jet**, titanium quartz

HELPFUL PEOPLE AND TRAVEL

Aquamarine, turquoise, **stibnite**, moonstone

Which crystals do I need in my home?

When choosing crystals to enhance your home, consider what you want from each room or area. What is the room used for? How do you want to feel in each space? For example, at different times the living room may function as a family room, home office, guest bedroom, or playroom. Consider the practical side of living in your home and the functions you wish to emphasize in your world. You will need a pen and paper for this exercise.

1 With the pen, roughly draw the floor plan of your home over the feng shui bagua map. For example, in the floor plan shown below, the bathroom is in the Wealth and Prosperity area. The kitchen-diner spans two bagua areas, and the living room and bedroom span three bagua areas (see key). If you have more than one story, do this for each floor.

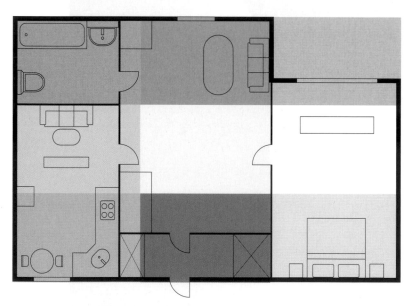

WEALTH AND PROSPERITY	FAME AND REPUTATION	LOVE AND MARRIAGE
HEALTH AND ANCESTORS	HEALTH AND CENTER	CHILDREN AND CREATIVITY
KNOWLEDGE AND SELF-CULTIVATION	CAREER AND LIFE PATH	HELPFUL PEOPLE AND TRAVELS

2 Select the crystals you need from The Crystal Finder (see pages 94–136) or from the bagua map (see page 27). Alternatively, you can intuitively choose the crystals you are drawn to—this is a flexible process that will evolve over time. With a little practice, when you focus your mind on a special purpose or area of your home, you will naturally notice the crystals you need. You can check your intuition with a pendulum (see page 98) and then look the crystals up in The Crystal Finder.

3 Once you have selected the crystals you're going to start with, place them around your home one room at a time. You may find that you don't have all the crystals you need to hand. I recommend you place the ones you do have immediately so they can start working and find or purchase any others to add later.

Select the crystals you are intuitively drawn to when focusing on a particular area or purpose of your home.

4 In each room, you will notice that some have obvious places where they need to be (they can be quite insistent on this) whereas other crystals will be happy wherever you place them. As you finish each room, take a few minutes to just be in the energy and be aware of how this room now feels. Is it different to how it felt before?

5 Continue placing the crystals around your home until you have completed the task. The crystals start working as soon as you place the first one with intent.

Crystals can change the energy in a room, from cheerful orange calcite (far left) to contemplative smoky quartz (left).

A room-by-room exploration

The size of your home doesn't matter. You may have a large house with each room having an individual use, or a studio apartment where a single space serves a multitude of purposes at different times.

I place citrine in every room to bring happiness and orange calcite which promotes laughter. I also like to protect my space by placing pyrite on every windowsill and by every door, to hold back external influences and disturbances. Tourmaline is my go-to crystal for personal protection. It acts as a shield keeping away unwanted energies.

You can also bring crystals into any room for specific occasions. For a party you might like crystals such as quartz for energy and orange calcite to bring fun and humor, whereas for a more somber occasion like a wake, smoky quartz to ease grief and unakite to appreciate what there really was and what could have been.

Crystals also make fabulous homeware gifts for all occasions. I know several couples who gave small crystal gifts to all their wedding guests—what a beautiful thing to do.

ENTRYWAY

I like the entrance to my home to be welcoming. I have a large, amethyst geode that greets visitors with a calm, relaxed, spiritual energy. A Buddha statue in my entryway holds a welcoming plate, which holds a changing selection of smaller crystals as the feeling takes me. These crystals are constantly refreshing the energy, so it always feels pleasant when you enter.

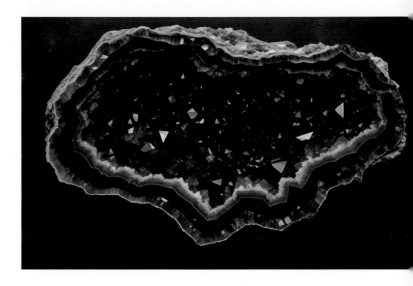

There's also tourmaline for protection and a large, citrine geode, which bring abundance into my home. If there are windows, you might like to place pyrite crystals on the windowsills, too, to hold back external influences and disturbances.

An amethyst geode (above) welcomes visitors to my home, while a Buddha statue in my entryway carries an offering plate (below), which can be filled with crystals that provide a refreshing energy.

LIVING ROOM

My living room is exactly that—a living room! Everything that doesn't happen in the kitchen happens in this room. So, it's a little chaotic and its function depends on the time of day and who is around.

A useful tip for a multifunctional room is to keep collections of crystals for different purposes to hand. This way, when the room is going to be used for a specific function, you can quickly pop these crystals around to help you focus on or relax into whatever you are doing. In my living room, there are large bowls of crystals for anyone to choose from and hold, to help both us and visitors as required. A quartz crystal geode, a quartz crystal ball, and a selenite lamp continuously cleanse the atmosphere from the happy but sometimes disparate energies of this multifunctional space.

The crystals you choose for the living room will depend on how you use the space. Much of my personal crystal collection resides in the living room, including several Lemurian quartz crystals. There is another welcoming, calming, and refreshing large amethyst geode, a large citrine crystal to bring joy and happiness, green calcite for calming, and rhodonite and celestite for musical creativity (as some of my music is written here too). There's petrified wood and a collection of prehistoric stone tools made of flint, which help keep us all grounded and connected to our ancestors. To help connect to spirit there's a quartz Buddha and a tektite. Then tourmaline again for protection in the form of a tourmaline medicine wheel.

There are various large crystals such as amethyst, fluorite, and pyrite on the windowsill as it helps reduce disturbances, such as noise, from outside the house (see page 81). We are lucky to have lovely neighbors; however, children playing, especially in the summer with all the windows open, can interfere with quiet times.

Lemurian quartz crystals boost happiness and bring a zest for life. They are good for rooms where you spend a lot of time, such as living rooms.

Positive and negative ions

Positive ions are released by most screens. They are the reason why you feel tired and low after you've spent too much time on your computer. Negative ions are naturally created with falling rain from a cloudburst, waterfalls, and crashing waves on a rocky shore. They make us feel up and awake.

A fluorite crystal or Himalayan salt lamp (shown right) near the television screen will help to absorb the positive ions emanating from it. You can employ crystal lamps like these, or selenite and other crystal lamps, to create calming lighting effects as well as receive the benefit of the crystalline energy throughout your home.

Quartz or granite work surfaces are a good way to introduce welcoming crystal energy into your kitchen.

KITCHEN

Do you cook? Or just heat food up? Is your kitchen a social place where friends chat or is the kitchen your private domain? Remember, there is no right and wrong. There is just whatever you want in your home.

If you would like to change the function of your kitchen, there are crystals that can help alter the energies to something more to your taste. To do this, start by bringing in crystals that will help you focus, such as fluorite and carnelian, while pyrite can help to hold back external influences and disturbances. Work surfaces made of quartz or granite are readily available. Granite has a high quantity of quartz in its structure. Quartz will help to energize and bring a happy and welcoming feel to your kitchen.

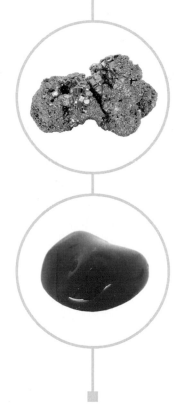

Pyrite (above right) will shield your kitchen from outside influences while carnelian (right) improves focus.

Some people can feel a bit spacey when they're cooking too, especially when using spicy ingredients. Try hematite, obsidian, and jet to keep you grounded. These are helpful crystals to have around you in any space or situation where you feel like this.

DINING ROOM

I love a crystal centerpiece on a formal dining table. It doesn't matter if it is a single, large crystal or a display made from many smaller crystals, it will have a similar effect. It will look amazing and bring energy and focus to everything, from the food to the conversation.

Obviously, any eating area should have crystals to help digestion (see box), but also think about some crystals to help people relax like amethyst and calcite, and to help the conversation flow, such as blue lace agate and kyanite.

Hematite (top), obsidian (center), and jet (bottom) will keep you grounded while cooking with spicy ingredients.

Crystals to aid digestion

Crystals that help digestion—including citrine, carnelian, tiger's eye, chrysocolla (top), peridot (center), lepidolite (bottom), labradorite, tourmaline, obsidian, pyrite, and many more—would work well in the kitchen and if you have a separate dining room or like TV dinners, then they'd be good there too! Ask your pendulum (see page 98) to help choose the best ones for you.

HOME OFFICE OR CREATIVE SPACE

Perhaps you have a permanent room dedicated to work, or this area may be overlap with another space, such as the kitchen table or dining room table, which becomes a temporary home office or creative area from time to time. Either way, it is all about productivity and focus.

When you are working from home it is so easy to be distracted, especially if you're working in a room that has other functions like your living room or kitchen. Fluorite can help you focus your mind, while snow quartz is great for clearing your mind from everything else that's going on in your home. A general tip for the workspace is to place quartz crystals around the room with all the terminations pointing towards the center to help keep your focus within the room. You can do this with at least four crystals, one in each corner of the room, or as many as you feel work for you, with no maximum limit.

Citrine brings abundance and is great for promoting Creativity (see page 52). Celestite, carnelian, and rhodonite are all good for creativity too, and pyrite for sparks of inspiration. If your "office" is an art studio, then add tiger's eye to the other creative and inspirational crystals too. Garnet, angelite, and hematite are all good for people who work with numbers (see page 50), which includes most people running their own business as well as accountants and other financial trades.

Rainbow fluorite (top) and snow quartz (above) bring focus to any workspace, whether you have your own home office or are working at the kitchen table.

Tourmaline (top) and pyrite (above) can protect your energy, or the energy of a room, from outside influences.

THERAPY ROOM OR MEDITATION SPACE

This room very much depends on the therapies you practice, so I'll assume you have all the relevant working crystals for your treatments. Besides these, I would suggest calming crystals such as calcites and amethyst. It's also nice to have two hand-size, green calcite crystals available to hold, which will quickly calm anyone who feels nervous. (They're magical to take to the dentist with you if you get anxious also!)

If you have clients coming into your home, crystals like tourmaline can provide protection, although it's probably best if you are wearing one for personal energy protection too. Place pyrite by any windows and doors.

Be aware of crystals around you when you book appointments for your clients. If you notice a specific crystal when you are on the phone or messaging with them, make sure that crystal is there with you when they come to see you. It might be for them, or you might find that you need it when they are with you!

Green calcite is a calming crystal, which can be held in the hand to feel its soothing energy.

Rhodochrosite (far left) and red tiger's eye (center) will invite passion into your sleeping area, while malachite (left) will ensure a good night's sleep.

BEDROOMS

What do you want from your bedroom? Do you desire a calm, peaceful, and relaxed night's sleep, vivid dreams that bring you the answers to your questions or problems, or a night of passion?

Rhodochrosite will ignite the flames of passion, while red tiger's eye can help you express your sexuality.

Malachite is my go-to crystal for sleep. If you tend to have disturbed sleep, try holding malachite for an hour before you go to bed. Pop the stone under your pillow or on your nightstand when you retire. Most people have improved sleep that night and if you continue with this method, you'll get better sleep each night until your sleep pattern goes back to normal in a couple of weeks. A big red jasper rock at the foot of your bed will help if you are affected by restless-leg syndrome causing interrupted sleep.

If you're not sleeping because of worries, then tourmaline is the answer to bring peace to your mind and a restful sleep. If your goal is to find answers in your dreams, then both celestite and lapis lazuli promote dreams and aid dream recall. Ruby will protect you from nightmares.

Ruby (top), amethyst (center), and smoky quartz (bottom) will ward away the bad dreams of children and adults alike.

In children's bedrooms, a large, blue calcite in the room is a good start. All the calcite family are calming, but I find children respond particularly well to the blue variety. As well as ruby mentioned on the previous page, amethyst and smoky quartz can also help prevent nightmares, while jade, mookaite, and spirit quartz can bring sweet dreams.

A selection of large, tumble polished stones in a bowl, including amethyst, blue calcite, hematite, lapis lazuli, aventurine, sodalite, strawberry quartz, red jasper, and kyanite, can be generally helpful to calm children, giving them a peaceful night's sleep and helping them to understand their dreams and be unafraid of them. Let them choose any of these crystals to hold and play with as they like. Children are naturally drawn to the crystals they need.

In guest bedrooms, any of the crystals for your own bedroom or the children's bedroom are fine. I would also add selenite to keep this room energetically cleansed for different guests and a selenite lamp can work well for this. Spirit quartz and rose quartz are also welcoming, suggesting that your guest is part of your family.

A selenite crystal lamp in the guest bedroom will cleanse the room's energy of previous visitors and create a fresh, welcoming energy for new guests.

BATHROOMS

Be aware that crystals placed in the lavatory, shower room, steam room, or sauna, such as selenite, vanadinite, halite, fuchsite, muscovite, celestite, and angelite, may react to water and dampness. Pyrite and hematite may rust while opal is vulnerable to drying out.

I have a soap dispenser made from petrified wood. You can also find them made from crystals in high-end stores. As well as dispensers and other accessories, you can buy sinks and even baths made from crystals, such as rose quartz, amethyst, fluorite, and quartz crystal.

STORAGE AREAS

Attics and lofts, large storage cupboards, garages, and basements can sometimes be damp. Consider the same warnings regarding crystals as for the bathroom section (above).

For these areas, you may want to consider crystals that can help to keep pests at bay, such as an elixir of amber (see page 15). Selenite can also help to keep the area cleansed and a quartz cluster will constantly refresh the energy. For security, consider tourmaline.

Take care to choose crystals for your bathroom decor that will not be damaged by steam. Rose quartz (right) and petrified wood (below) can be made into beautiful bathroom accessories.

Opposite: Crystals, especially rose quartz, bring a loving energy to your garden.

OUTDOOR AREAS

Whether you have a garden or backyard, patio, balcony, or even just a windowsill, you can incorporate crystals into your outside space.

Something I am often asked is what you should do with broken crystals? I believe that they should go back to the ground where they've come from. The earth will reenergize them, and the plants will adore them. If you really love a crystal that breaks and want to still keep it near you, you can pop it in a plant pot indoors.

Plants love crystals! I always plant a crystal, or place nearby on the soil, whenever I bed in a new plant. The crystal varies from one plant to another, but generally clear quartz will help everything grow. My garden is surrounded with rose quartz rocks defining the flower beds, with crystals, rough rocks, and tumble polished stones everywhere. Rose quartz brings a loving feeling to the whole garden, which helps plant thrive.

Today there is a widely available choice of outdoor furniture such as tables and chairs. Some years ago in Florence, Italy, I saw a beautiful desk made completely from three massive quartz crystals! Any quartz—including rose quartz, quartz, petrified wood, agate, and jasper—will work well as garden furniture, because they bring the energy of the crystal into your garden.

Many varieties of quartz, such as rose quartz and agate (above), can be made into beautiful garden furniture, which will bring energy into the garden.

Chakras in the home

Chakras are the body's energy "hot spots." They occur where there is a natural accumulation of energy in the body and are the easiest places to exchange energy with the world around you. Your home is an extension of your energy and also has chakras, or energy "hot spots."

Chakra is a Sanskrit word meaning "wheel." Whereas, in reality, chakras are more like spinning, flowing, fluxing balls of energy than a simple circle. Various Vedic traditions suggest there are many major energy centers numbering from 3 to 24, but in this exercise (see box below), we will focus on the system with seven major chakras, which is most followed in the West.

Identifying your home's chakras

The location of the chakras within each person's home will vary because they reflect your own energy, and how you use the different rooms and areas in your home. For example, the Base chakra is connected to the ground. This may be a basement or outbuilding, utility room, or bathroom with pipes running underground (even if you're in a high-rise apartment). You can identify the chakras in your home with your pendulum (see page 98).

1 Take a few deep breaths and still your mind.
2 Holding your pendulum out in front of you, walk slowly around your home. As you walk, ask your pendulum: "Am I in my home's base chakra?"
3 You will receive a positive answer when your pendulum gives you a "yes" response (see page 98).
4 Ask for the next chakra, and repeat steps 1–3 until you identify all seven.
5 Place the corresponding crystals in this room or area (see chart opposite or The Crystal Finder, pages 94–136, for more options).

The chakra areas

The chakra areas of the home shown below are a guide. Don't be surprised to find your home differs from these, that's normal. If you live in a studio apartment, then you will still find different areas which will house the chakras.

BASE
Location: Basement, outbuilding, utility room, bathroom or toilet with pipes running underground, garden.
Keywords: Survival, connection, security, nurture, passion, endings, new beginnings.
Crystals: Red jasper, obsidian, smoky quartz, jet.
Color: Red.

SACRAL
Location: Creative rooms, home office, workshop, workplace, or areas sometimes used for this purpose, such as the kitchen table.
Keywords: Connection to people, creativity, energy, sex, fertility, happiness.
Crystals: Carnelian, orange calcite, copper, moonstone.
Color: Orange.

SOLAR PLEXUS
Location: Living room, family room, bathroom, kitchen.
Keywords: Personal power, self-esteem, learning, concentration, adaptability.
Crystals: Citrine, amber, tiger's eye.
Color: Yellow.

HEART
Location: Kitchen (hearth), dining area, living room.
Keywords: Love, adventure, relationships, commitment, compassion, hope, beauty (seeing and feeling), harmony.
Crystals: Malachite, rose quartz, aventurine, emerald.
Color: Green.

THROAT
Location: Study, home office, living room, family room.
Keywords: Communication, expression, freedom (especially from addiction), choice, faith, decisions, leadership.
Crystals: Blue lace agate, turquoise, blue chalcedony, kyanite.
Color: Blue.

BROW
Location: Library, meditation or treatment room, living room, den, home office, bedroom, garden.
Keywords: Mind, ideas, dreams, psychic abilities, truth, intellect, teaching, feelings of adequacy.
Crystals: Lapis lazuli, sodalite, celestite, sapphire.
Color: Indigo

CROWN
Location: Front door, bedroom, attic, rooftop.
Keywords: Openness, connection, spirituality, awareness, trust, selflessness, inspiration, originality, fulfillment.
Crystals: Amethyst, labradorite, Herkimer diamond, selenite.
Color: Violet.

Chapter 3

Crystals at Work

Crystal well-being at work 46

Working from home 52

Office-based working 53

Warehouses and factories 59

Working with the public 62

Traveling for work and commuting 65

Crystal well-being at work

Most people spend a third of their lives or more working. So, to ignore the contribution that crystals can make to your everyday living, health, and well-being at work is a significant omission.

You may already know exactly which crystals you would like to have with you in your workplace—maybe you even have a separate collection in your office—but various situations can occur in different types of working environments. If you feel uncertain about which crystals you might need with you in your place of work, there are plenty of ideas on the following pages.

Bringing crystals into your working environment can enhance your daily life in a myriad of ways.

Job satisfaction

Whether you work for a company or for yourself, whether you work at home, in an office, or all around the world, enjoying what you do is so very important for your health and welfare. Job satisfaction—seeing the benefit of your work to yourself and others—can lift your spirit and bring you joy. When it's lacking, it can bring you down and make you physically and emotionally susceptible to illness. If you find that you're not enjoying your work, try any or all the following:

- **Red jasper** to support your immune system and help to keep you well.
- **Orange calcite** to keep you calm and bring a smile back to your face. Don't be surprised if you start laughing again!
- **Golden healer quartz** will help to heal your inner self and find satisfaction within.
- **Chrysoprase** can let you see through any confusion in your mind. Perhaps it will help you to decide if you want to change what you are doing or the way you are doing it.
- **Celestite** connects you to the dreams you might have lost along the way.
- **Snow quartz** will give you clarity.
- **Amethyst** helps your soul tell you what's good for your spirit.

From top: Red jasper, orange calcite, golden healer quartz, chrysoprase, celestite, snow quartz, and amethyst all promote job satisfaction in different ways.

BRINGING CRYSTALS INTO THE WORKPLACE

There are a few reasons why people don't take crystals to work. For example, company policy may prohibit wearing jewelry or personal symbols or perhaps you are afraid of your crystals being lost or stolen. But the reason I hear—far more often than all the others put together—is embarrassment about what others might think or say.

Crystals do indeed work in weird and wondrous ways—but you must have them with you and let them do their stuff. If you are worried about what your work colleagues will think, start off with a tourmaline crystal. This will help you to worry less about the opinions of others and gradually build the confidence to bring more crystals with you to work. You can also wear crystals as jewelry beneath your clothes, or carry them in your pockets, a pouch, or around your neck in a bag. In this way, no one really needs to know that you have them with you at all.

Prejudice can happen in any work environment (see box opposite) and can raise its head wherever there is someone different. And yet it is possibly because you are different that you were hired in the first place! Many people have a superficial desire to fit in at work, but this path does not lead to happiness or job fulfillment and satisfaction. So firstly, celebrate your uniqueness and individuality, wear tourmaline, and worry less. Then slowly add crystals to your environment. Of course, if you already feel happy and confident in yourself, then take your crystals on day one and proudly place them on your desk!

Tourmaline will give you the confidence to bring your crystals into work and proudly place them on your desk.

The power of tourmaline

A number of years back, I was working with a client on the issues she faced in her male-dominated work environment. There was a general, low-level sense of misogyny in the company and one man in particular was giving her a hard time because "it wasn't a place for a woman." She felt she couldn't take crystals to her workplace as she'd be ridiculed. I suggested she wear a tourmaline crystal pendant on a chain, long enough to wear under her clothes so it couldn't be seen. Among many other things, tourmaline helps us worry less about what others think. It is also a very protective crystal. It can be magically life-changing for some people.

I suggested that she wear tourmaline every day and night for two weeks, and when she came for her next session, she'd been feeling confident enough to take a few crystals into work. All except one of her work colleagues had been open to them, were interested in which crystal does what, and some had even asked if she could get them a crystal to help with one thing or another.

The exception was her misogynistic colleague, who was being more coarse and vulgar as each day went by. One day, he cornered her when she was alone in the office kitchen and she feared the worst as he menacingly approached. Something made her hold her tourmaline pendant, which she was now wearing openly on top of her clothes. As she held it, he broke down in tears and apologized for giving her such a hard time. He explained that he was having marital difficulties—and even asked if she could get him a crystal that would help!

Tourmaline (right) can be made into beautiful jewelry (above right), making it easy to wear in the workplace.

Numeracy

Numeracy in any occupation can be helped with garnet, angelite, and hematite (below). Wear or carry any or all of these when you're working with numbers.

WORK–LIFE BALANCE

Work–life balance is a massive challenge for anyone who is self-employed, works from home, or is completely committed to their job. Even if you LOVE what you do, your mind, body, and soul need to rest, relax, and recuperate so you can revitalize and approach your work refreshed and reenergized.

Start your day with a crystal meditation every morning (see opposite). You will quickly find yourself relaxed and energized, with more focus and more time for both work and play.

Rose quartz promotes love and care in all relationships, and so is the ideal crystal companion to remind you of the importance of self-care when planning your day and maintaining a healthy work-life balance.

Schedule a healthy work-life balance by taking time to refresh and revitalize with crystals.

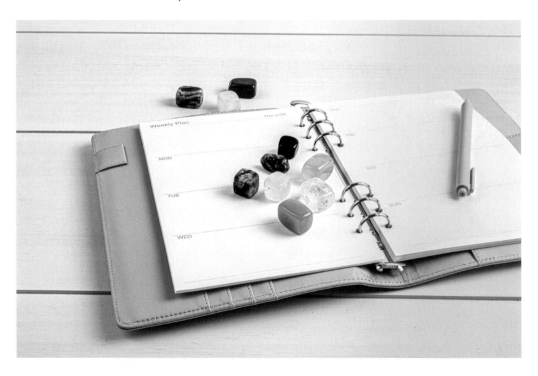

Quartz crystal meditation

For the best results, do this exercise daily, even on non-workdays. You only need 10 minutes, maybe less.

1 Hold your quartz crystal in front of you. Take three slow, deep breaths in through your nose and out through your mouth.

2 Look at the crystal and notice everything you can about it—how it looks, its shape, including the shape of the termination (the point) at the end, and the play of color inside as the light hits it from different angles.

3 Close your eyes and explore the crystal with your fingertips. Become aware of the flat areas, sharp and pointy bits, the spots that feel hard or soft, and the rough and smooth parts.

4 Feel the energy of the crystal. Be conscious of any sensations inside your body and mind.

5 Focus on one thought. Imagine this thought traveling out of your mind, through your Third Eye (Brow chakra), and straight into your quartz crystal. See the thought transform to a bright light inside the crystal, and then watch as the bright light is directed through the point and up into the sky above you. See it going farther and farther away until it is a tiny dot way up above you, that finally vanishes.

6 Focus on any other thoughts in your head and do the same thing, letting them go one at a time until there are no more thoughts left. Your mind is clear, open, and free to focus on your day.

For those juggling with work-life balance, a daily quartz crystal meditation can bring you the energy and focus you need to tackle your day.

Working from home

In today's world, many people can carry out their jobs from home. Many of the crystals that can help you in an office environment, such as kyanite for communication or fluorite to counter the negative effects of screens, will also help you at your desk or kitchen table at home.

While lots of people in the creative industries, such as artists or designers, may have their own studios or workshops in an area of their home, there are also many who access the technology they need online to complete their roles. Whether your work is financial and numerical or creative and artistic, you may need hematite to keep you grounded when you are working from home.

Creativity

Crystals such as amazonite (right), ametrine (center), aventurine (below right), azurite, obsidian, bloodstone, celestite, chrysocolla, citrine, mookaite, moonstone, pink banded agate, rose quartz, ruby, sodalite, tourmaline, and yellow fluorite (below) can inspire creativity.

Office-based working

There are many crystals that work well in an office environment. On the following pages, I also cover some of the challenges you might face in this kind of workplace and suggest crystals that can help you.

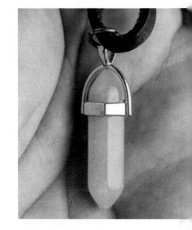

When any workplace works well it can be like a team or a family. Each person has their own character and their own role, but overall the needs of the group are paramount. Bring spirit quartz to your workplace to help bond the team. It's a great crystal to have when you are working with other people as it promotes a family atmosphere amongst coworkers.

Be productive! Crystals such as citrine and carnelian can bring creative energy, pyrite carries sparks of inspiration, and rhodonite can promote artistry. Whereas red jasper and hematite will keep you grounded and purple fluorite and sodalite will help you to focus on your objectives. Celestite and yellow fluorite will support you in these goals.

Keep a large aventurine tumble stone on your desk, or nearby wherever you are working, and hold it when you feel unmotivated and want to feel more inspired.

Purple fluorite (top) brings focus to the workplace, while holding aventurine (above) will help to spark motivation.

OVERCOMING OFFICE CHALLENGES

Office environments can be challenging for some. It is not always obvious or intended that stressful conditions are created—sometimes things just happen and it's not until the situation starts to affect people harmfully that the mental strain becomes apparent. Mental health can be either supported or adversely affected in the workplace. Some companies and environments are super supportive of people going through tough challenges outside of work while others expect you to just get on with your job. Crystals such as lepidolite and kunzite can help you focus on and change work patterns which are unhealthy for both you and your co-workers. Sugilite and charoite can help any individual in the team going through a rough time mentally, either at work or outside the office environment.

If there is a bully in your office, carry or wear tiger's eye to give you courage. Hold it when you feel threatened. Keep tourmaline with you to help you worry less about what other people think and also to avoid the self-limiting trap of victim mentality.

Lepidolite (top) and kunzite (above) will help you set healthy working patterns.

TECHNICAL CHALLENGES

Technology can be a fantastic asset in the workplace. Not just for big corporations but also for smaller business and the self-employed. It can free up time and energy spent on mundane operations as well as boost creativity and productivity. However, when things go wrong with tech, it can be the most frustrating part of your day!

If things start to go wrong, keep calm and grab a calcite crystal. If you're panicking, go for green calcite, but calcite is such a calming crystal that any color you have to hand will help. Once you are in a calm place, garnet, angelite, and hematite all help to link your left and right brain, helping you to see things from all angles simultaneously. They channel insight and intuition, helping you to work things out based on mathematics and practicalities, and find both logical and creative answers to problems.

Problem solve by linking the left and right sides of your brain with garnet (top), angelite (center), and hematite (bottom).

The power of fluorite

Whether you are working in an office or from home, if you spend a lot of time on your computer then you're likely to suffer from screen fatigue. This is caused when positive ions are given off by your computer screen, which can make us feel tired and low. Over time this can cause other issues, such as depression and insomnia. Negative ions occur wherever there is lots of crashing water, like waves on a rocky seashore. It's one of the main reasons why you feel refreshed after a shower. Fluorite is naturally jam-packed full of negative ions (in fact, far too many). As soon as there is an excess of positive ions in the atmosphere making you feel low, fluorite crystals can suck them up and radiate negative ions that make you feel refreshed and awake.

Purple fluorite (above) can negate the positive ions coming from computer screens. Like waves crashing on the shore, it will release negative ions that will wake you up and make you feel refreshed.

COMMUNICATION

"Talk your talk" and tell people what you really think! Whether you are an employer, an employee, a business partner, or a work colleague, there are a myriad of reasons that you may feel communicatively stifled. For example, you may want to avoid upsetting or offending someone, you don't want to be wrong, or you feel embarrassed. In any of these situations, kyanite is your go-to crystal. It will give you the inner strength and communicative skill needed to tell it how it is.

Aquamarine and lapis lazuli can help you focus and communicate clearly, while with mookaite you will find it easier to speak kindly in difficult situations.

If you feel people are not hearing you or listening to your ideas, the office can be a frustrating place. Getting more and more het up is not going to help you. Blue lace agate and howlite bring a calming, communicative vibe to how you say things and put your ideas across to your colleagues.

Some people find it difficult to share their emotions in the workplace. They may feel it's inappropriate, embarrassing, or would create an awkward atmosphere. Blue chalcedony, which eases trauma, can help to release emotions and share them in a way people will better understand, so your colleagues can be supportive.

If you feel uncomfortable about speaking in public, then turquoise, septarian, and amethyst are recommended for confidence and clarity. If you're suffering from physical issues that limit your communication such as laryngitis, a throat infection, sore throat, and so on, then blue calcite will help. Amethyst is good for bacterial infections and carnelian for viral infections. Carry these with you and hold them when you need to speak.

Be calm and communicative with your colleagues with howlite (above left) and blue lace agate (left).

CONFLICT

You can't avoid disagreements at work. Assuming that there are two or more people working in the office, then at times disagreements will happen, whether it is with employers, staff, partners, coworkers, suppliers, customers, clients—or even yourself, if you wear many hats in your own business!

The important thing is to disagree and discuss in a constructive way, so that in the end everyone is happy with the outcome. Raised voices and insults don't solve problems; they only create more to deal with later. There are a few techniques you can try with crystals. Firstly, bring an amethyst crystal cluster into your workplace. It will instantly start to create a better, easier, and more co-operative atmosphere. Rose quartz can quell the quarrelsome tendencies of difficult colleagues and ease the situation. Kunzite will help to release bad feelings that people might be holding on to after a dispute.

An amethyst crystal cluster in your office or workplace will soothe a quarrelsome atmosphere.

The power of quartz

Energy doesn't miraculously disappear—it's always an exchange between one type and another. While debate in the workplace can be productive, it will sometimes leave an unpleasant feeling, anger, or discombobulated energy in the room.

Place a quartz crystal ball (shown right) anywhere in the office to absorb any uncomfortable atmosphere caused by jealousy or any other kind of workplace challenge. You will need to cleanse it every day to clear any negative energy it has picked up. At the end of each day, hold it under running water for a minute or two to wash away any unhelpful energy it has collected (see page 20–21 for other simple ways to cleanse your crystals.) When you cleanse the crystal ball you are exchanging positive clear energy for any negativity it has picked up. If you don't, then it will eventually release it back into the room.

THROWN IN AT THE DEEP END

Sometimes it can feel like you are thrown in at the deep end at work. You're asked to do something, and you just haven't been shown how to do it. The magical crystal that can help is purple fluorite. All varieties of fluorite crystals help to focus the mind, but the purple variety also improves cognitive ability, especially when you are feeling stressed. It will activate your left brain (the logical side), helping you to focus, function, and work things out. It will also let you clearly see if you are completely out of your depth and really do need a hand from a coworker or manager.

Fluorite helps to focus your mind.

Warehouses and factories

From repetitive tasks to noisy and disruptive sounds, working environments like warehouses and factories can be among the most challenging.

Meditate with a rhodonite stone to help you cope with noisy or repetitive workplace activities.

Monotonous actions and noise both have their own natural rhythm, which you can treat as a meditation. Like all meditations, if you add a crystal to the process, you will find that it becomes much easier to find inner stillness and peace.

Hold a rhodonite stone (if it is not practical to hold the crystal, pop it in your pocket or bra so you can feel it with your body). As you carry out a repetitive task, become aware of your breath and allow it to naturally synchronize with your movement. You can do the same thing with noise. Hold your rhodonite and allow your breath to harmonize with the tempo of the sounds around you. Don't try and force it, just be with it.

You might feel a pulsing in the stone you're holding. Become aware of its vibration. You will quickly find that once-disruptive sounds or monotonous actions become calming and strangely relaxing.

CHALLENGING WORKPLACE ENVIRONMENTS

There are many reasons why we might find our physical place of work challenging. For example, emotional issues, like items that remind you of a painful time; personal challenges, such as colors that make you feel uncomfortable, stifled, or unproductive; or physical issues, like the layout of the space, noise, or allergenic materials. Whether the source of your discomfort is personal or environmental, there are crystal ways to help.

Simply add pleasing crystals to offset anything you find uncomfortable. If you are not sure which crystals to choose, you can ask your pendulum for help (see page 98) or check The Crystal Finder (see page 94–136) for specific problems or situations.

Make your workplace environment work for you

If you feel uneasy in your physical workspace, the following exercise will help you to identify what may be causing the disruption. By placing the crystals as suggested, you will be amazed how things change, either in how you feel or what happens to the layout of the room!

1 Sit quietly in the space. It's always better to do this during active work time, if possible, to recognize the effect others might be having on you, too. Close your eyes.

2 Recognize the sounds around you. Focus on each one individually and notice how it affects you. For any sounds that create a discordant sensation, place a pyrite crystal in the direction it's coming from.

3 Open your eyes and be aware of anything you see that gives you an uncomfortable feeling inside. If it's a shape, then place a crystal pyramid in that direction to change the potential

Pyrite (above) can help to ease disruption from noisy or discordant sounds in the workplace.

A crystal pyramid will deflect any uncomfortable energy you sense coming from a cluttered environment.

energy created by the shape. A cluttered area can be dealt with simply by tidying (or if it's someone else's possessions, explain to them how it is affecting you and ask them to tidy it). Color is easy to deal with— just add a crystal of a hue you like, to give you a more pleasing aspect.

4   To deal with people who are causing a problem, place a smoky quartz crystal pointing toward them to send back any energy which is upsetting you.

5   If the layout of the space is uncomfortable and you cannot change it, arrange some small crystals in a layout you would like the room to have. In the middle, place a standing, clear quartz crystal or a fluorite crystal for focus.

Arrange crystals in a layout you would like your workplace to have.

A smoky quartz crystal (right) will redirect negative energy back toward those who are causing a problem.

Working with the public

Protect personal energy with (from top) tourmaline, turquoise, calcite, and carnelian.

The benefits of working with, on behalf of, or caring for others can be manifold and rewarding. However, for any activity that involves working with people, think about protecting yourself first and foremost.

Protect your personal energy with tourmaline, your spiritual energy with turquoise, your emotions with calcite, and your physical health with carnelian, which protects against illness.

CUSTOMER SERVICES AND SALES

At some point in these professions, you will almost certainly deal with people who are not happy with the service or product they have received. Few customers return to say how happy they are! Do not take their stuff on. Anything they say is not personal to you. They are expressing their anger, fear, or frustration with the product, or service they have received in the chain before you. Wear tourmaline to protect against worrying about what they think about you. Then you will be able to fulfill your role in a way that will help the customer, your employer—and your sanity!

Telephone sales or services are types of job where it can be especially difficult to maintain focus through long hours. I've already covered many of the crystals that could be helpful (see page 35), whether you are working from home or in a call center. Keep a fluorite crystal on your desk and either hold it or focus on it when your attention drifts. You can also place a grid of four quartz crystals—one on each corner of your workstation, pointing toward the center of the desk—to increase focus. If you are feeling scattered before you start work, try holding carnelian for five minutes before you begin. It will help to pull in your emotional edges, and you will be much more productive.

CARING PROFESSIONS

It does not matter what modalities you are trained in, or where or how you work, crystals can help both you and those you are treating or taking care of. Crystals can help your clients to feel calm and relaxed as soon as they arrive. Crystals can help you stay focused, protecting your energy from your client's issues. You can even employ crystals as massage tools, as talking points, or any other examples you can think of.

Although there are so many crystals that can help in different ways, the most important crystal for your clients must be calcite. Any color calcite, as they are all calming.

For you, tourmaline, or another crystal you feel drawn to, is essential for protection. Other essential crystals in your space are amethyst for spiritual connection and calm energy, rose quartz for love and friendship, a quartz crystal ball or cluster to keep the energy refreshed, selenite for cleansing, fluorite for focus, kyanite for communication, and rhodochrosite for passion.

Crystals, such as rose quartz, can be incorporated into the workplace as massage tools.

Perhaps the most important thing to remember, wherever you work and whatever you do, is that if you notice a crystal in any way, then you need that crystal either for your benefit, or for your client's. If you feel drawn to it and like the look of it or its feel, you should have it in your treatment room. If you are repulsed, dislike the look, or it makes you feel uneasy, you also need it, and possibly more so.

All colors of calcite are calming for both you and the ones you are caring for.

Traveling for work and commuting

Traveling for work can be either a positive or negative experience. Commuting may be seen as an energy hole that drains your soul, or you can treat it as an opportunity for time and space at the beginning and end of your day. Similarly, travel can be a physical, emotional, and mental drain on your being, or you can treat it as a fantastic opportunity to meet people and see the world.

Turquoise and aquamarine are traditional protection crystals for travelers. So, carry or wear one or both crystals whenever you're on the move.

Bowenite is another amazing crystal. It is wonderful for promoting adventure, brings success in business, and focuses on your personal goals and ambitions. Bowenite removes blocks you put in your own way, giving you the freedom to travel your own path.

If you're a traveling salesperson, whether at a global or corporate level, or selling at local events like health fairs and music festivals, then citrine is a must. It will bring successful sales and abundance, both financially and experientially.

Bowenite (below left) and citrine (below right) bring success in business and are a must for anyone traveling for work.

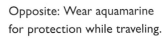

Opposite: Wear aquamarine for protection while traveling.

Crystal travel kit

Whenever I travel, I like to carry a small crystal "first aid" kit with me. Because of the weight restrictions on flights, I carry mostly small crystals that can be helpful in multiple ways.

I carry or wear tourmaline, aquamarine, and turquoise for protection—the turquoise and aquamarine doubling up with kyanite to aid communication, especially when traveling in lands with unfamiliar customs and languages. Citrine promotes joy and abundance of experiences and is also helpful for any tummy upsets from time changes or unusual foods. Amethyst and carnelian keep infections at bay. A couple of other helpful crystals to have on board are banded amethyst for pain and bloodstone for any minor injuries. A quartz crystal and citrine can aid these too.

Lemurian quartz crystal

Amethyst

Lapis lazuli

Blue lace agate

I also like to carry a crystal chakra set. My travel chakra kit includes red jasper, carnelian, citrine, malachite, blue lace agate (or blue chalcedony if blue lace agate is unavailable), lapis lazuli, amethyst, and a small Lemurian quartz crystal as a master crystal. I find the Lemurian crystals so powerful that you can often employ a smaller crystal with amazing effects, making them ideal for carrying with you when you are traveling.

Kyanite (above right) works well with aquamarine (center) and turquoise (right) to aid communication on any journey.

Malachite

Citrine

Carnelian

Red jasper

Chapter 4

Lifestyle Crystals

Crystals for life 70

Relationships 78

Career and study 82

Emotional well-being 86

Spiritual well-being 92

Crystals for life

Crystals can help with so many of the things that happen in daily life, from nurturing relationships to career goals, and there are crystals that can assist you in anything you are attempting to achieve and help to ease your path.

Quartz crystal brings a feel-good enthusiasm for life, whatever direction you choose on your life path.

Whatever crystals you choose to help you on your life path, quartz crystal will give you a zest for life, boosting your enthusiasm to live life to the full! When you are feeling good, your quality of life improves. This is one of the fundamental keys to the doorway to happiness, health, and well-being.

The following pages offer a myriad of crystals for improving your quality of life, whether you are struggling with choices on your life's path, need a little luck or inspiration, or simply wish to elevate your mood on a day-to-day basis.

Feel-good crystals

If life is a party, then jasper is the DJ! Jasper (top) is a mood elevator and is renowned as a general tonic for keeping you well when you are feeling good. Amazonite, calcite, carnelian, chrysocolla, chrysoprase, copper (center), lepidolite, peridot (bottom), and quartz crystal are all crystals which make you feel good.

BEING PRESENT

Live in the moment—it is the only moment that exists! The past has gone and the future is not yet here, so do not dwell on them.

We see our past through different filters as we age, grow, and spiritually develop. A wise man once told me a story about living in the moment. He described a ship crossing an ocean. We create our past, just as the ship creates the wake of the ocean stretching out behind. The future stretches out before us like the endless sea in front of the ship. The only thing that exists in this moment is the ship, and the actions we take in this moment to move forward, creating the wake. The future is always an unknown, open ocean of possibility.

Unakite will help your mind stay in the present moment and merlinite will help you to seize it.

Above: Unakite (top) and merlinite (above) will help you to live and act in the present moment.

GRATITUDE

The joy of appreciation is beneficial to a healthy lifestyle. It is always good to remember that there is beauty in everything, even if things do not seem that way at first sight, and noticing this will bring a smile to your face every day. Cobaltoan calcite is a magical crystal that will help you see the beauty in your world. It promotes gratitude toward people, your environment, and the Universe.

Magical cobaltoan calcite will help you to see the beauty in everything around you.

NEW CHALLENGES

What to one person may seem like a giant leap, another might view simply as a small step. When I think about challenges, I always remind myself that there is no right or wrong. If you feel challenged by any new situation, then you are.

Crystals like Herkimer diamond (above) can help you take the leap into new beginnings and challenges.

Tourmaline will give you the strength and the courage you need to face any new challenge. It will open your mind to the positive benefits of any situation and help you see the way forward. Any new beginning—whether a new project, a new relationship, or a new job—is also helped with citrine, Herkimer diamond, moonstone, ruby, and tiger's eye, too.

CHANGE

All change is good, but we do not always see it that way when we are going through it. I like American author Richard Bach's observation that: "What the caterpillar calls the end of the world, the Master calls a butterfly" (see Resources, page 137). Yes, sometimes change can be uncomfortable—even painful—but oh, how wondrous change is. There are several crystals that can help you through the process of change if you are feeling challenged.

If you are feeling stuck and want to make changes, but you do not know where or how to start, then let lepidolite, ruby, or bowenite show you the way. Ametrine also allows you to see the changes to your lifestyle that are needed and facilitates the transformation within you that change brings. Amethyst eases the process of change and moonstone soothes your emotions, gently bathing your heart center in healing energy.

There are a few life events, such as divorce or moving home, which are particularly challenging for most people who experience them. For these really momentous changes in your life, titanium quartz can help you see the situation and its many possibilities from different angles. Garnet can ease these difficult times, helping you to remain rational and composed, while green calcite is great for keeping you calm. If disputes occur during this process, rainbow fluorite can help you resolve them, kunzite brings ease to calm the atmosphere after a disagreement, and jade will help to bring justice to the situation.

But my go-to crystal in these situations is always a Lemurian quartz crystal. It is as if it has the wisdom and knowledge of how to cope, to be your friend, and simply be with you during troubled times.

Garnet will help you to keep your cool during life's big changes, such as moving home.

COMMUNICATION

Whether you are expressing your feelings to a friend or presenting in a public auditorium, communicating your ideas and beliefs is important. It does not matter if you do this through speech, the written word, art, media, or any other creative modality, as long as you do it. There are many crystals that can aid and inspire Creativity (see box, page 52), which may help you to express yourself in a way that suits you.

Sometimes our channels of communication may be blocked, perhaps by a physical issue or our emotional past. Maybe you don't want to upset someone with what you are telling them or you do not want to draw attention to yourself. There really are endless possibilities and there are many crystals that can help in all sorts of ways (see box, opposite). There is also more information about crystals for Communication in Chapter 3 (see page 56).

DECISION MAKING

Some people find making decisions a bit tricky, very difficult, or even absolutely impossible. This is especially true when there are too many options to choose from. Muscovite can help! Just like your inner pendulum (see page 98), it acts as a mirror, reflecting your innermost feelings and helping you to make even the toughest decisions in life. Traditionally, jade brings wisdom, while crystals such as amethyst and citrine can also help you make wise choices.

Sometimes decisions are not an obvious choice between one thing and another. There may be many options or a combination of solutions. Tourmalinated quartz illuminates the possible paths before you while aragonite allows you to see things from multiple viewpoints.

To make it easier to select an outcome, aventurine calms the mind, fluorite will help you to focus on the issues, and mookaite will support you while you find creative solutions. Ruby helps with matters of the heart and pink banded agate holds a gentle, loving energy. Crystals like amber help you to tap into past experiences, while stibnite brings the wisdom of teachers and past masters. Banded amethyst can take the pain away from the decision-making process.

In their own unique ways, all these crystals help you find answers to life's problems.

Express yourself

There are many crystals that can help you communicate, each in their own unique way. Which of these crystals are you intuitively drawn to? If you do not think that you are an intuitive soul, then ask your pendulum to help you choose (see page 98).

Angelite

Blue apatite

Aqua aura

Aquamarine

Howlite

Mookaite

Blue calcite

Kyanite

Purple Mexican fluorite

Blue chalcedony

Lapis lazuli

Blue sodalite

Blue lace agate

Amethyst

Turquoise

Septarian

Smoky quartz

FLOW

Many spiritual traditions around the world compare energy to water (see Feng Shui, pages 26–29). One Taoist thought offers the idea that this *chi* energy flows like a river. When you move with the current in the river's downstream flow, everything is easy and your journey flows quickly and safely. However, if you try to move against the current, it is much harder to reach your goal. The farther upstream you get, the tougher your task, and eventually you become too tired and exhausted to continue, leaving you stranded or worse.

When your life flows, you feel good and abundance flows. Amethyst, aquamarine, charoite, garnet, kunzite, merlinite, mookaite, rhodochrosite, smoky quartz, and spirit quartz all help to make everything flow better in your life. Things that were "stuck" become fluid. Your life moves forward.

Different crystals work in various amazing ways, always working on the underlying causes and not necessarily the symptoms. So, sometimes, crystals can be a bit of a trial-and-error experiment. Use your intuition or your pendulum (see page 98) to select the best crystal for you, or simply give each one a go for a couple of weeks and see how your life changes.

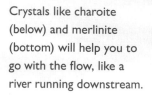

Crystals like charoite (below) and merlinite (bottom) will help you to go with the flow, like a river running downstream.

INSPIRATION

Allow the flow of brainwaves to unshackle sparks of genius from your mind. Ametrine, carnelian, fire agate, labradorite, orange calcite, and tourmaline can all help to free your mind. Opal and rose quartz allow your imagination to flow freely, while pyrite creates flashes of inspiration to add to the mix.

These crystals benefit further from the addition of tourmalinated quartz and rutilated quartz, which promote lateral thinking. Morganite allows you to take the initiative and bring your ideas to the fore.

Being true to yourself is essential in many ways and when you are expressing yourself or being creative, it is important to be inspired from your soul. Individuality and uniqueness are supported by azurite.

Certain crystals, such as fire agate (above), can free your mind, while others, such as pyrite, will offer flashes of inspiration, and so are helpful in creative endeavors.

LUCK

From time to time, we all need a little good fortune in our lives. Many diverse cultures around the world have traditional and historical beliefs attached to the crystals that are naturally available in their region. However, I have found that moonstone, tiger's eye, and turquoise work well in bringing a bit of luck that can tip the scales in your favor.

Relationships

Rose quartz is the crystal of love. It promotes beauty and helps you to feel better about yourself—the most important relationship of all! Self-love is the key to inner beauty, and it is this inner self which glows, radiating your loveliness to others.

Rose quartz is a great crystal for friendship and will help you to nurture the special relationships in your life. Friendship is a special thing, a bond between two people that might last forever. However, there may come a time when you need to make new friends. Maybe you have moved to a new town or have changed careers. While you are adjusting to your new life and facing changes (see page 73), it always helps to welcome new people into your life. Take bowenite with you everywhere, give rose quartz to people you like who may become a friend, and wear turquoise to show you are open to communication.

Morganite will help you see the beauty inside people—if you hold this crystal when meeting new people, you will quickly discover their true nature. If you do not want to be noticed doing this, keep it in your pocket where you can access it unseen.

Kyanite, which eases networking, can help you connect to people. Danburite helps you mix with others (see box, opposite). Some people find it difficult to express their best features and share their good qualities with others. Aquamarine can support you as you bring forth your best characteristics and step into your power, recognizing your inner talents and beauty.

Rose quartz (above right) is the crystal of love and will help you to nurture the special relationships in your life.

FINDING LOVE

Rose quartz is renowned as the stone of love and romance, although it works for any kind or relationship, including friendship. There are several other crystals that can help you with love too, such as rhodochrosite, which brings passion into any relationship, and celestite, which can help you to connect from your heart.

If you dream of love but do not find it, rhodonite grounds your love in the physical world and will aid your search for the right partner. Hematite and stibnite attract new partners. Citrine, dalmatian stone, fluorite, and lapis lazuli promote healthy, loving relationships. Agate and stibnite promote faithfulness and marriage or partnership. Sexuality may be liberated with copper. Chrysocolla revitalizes and morganite repairs existing relationships. For existing connections that need a refresh, turquoise can bring a spark of romance into an old relationship, while charoite will help you to let old relationships go.

Bring passion into your relationships with rhodochrosite.

The power of danburite

Danburite helps you mix with others. I remember one of my students who went on to be a Master Teacher was also a hypnotherapist. She combined crystal healing with hypnotherapy in her practice. She had a client who found it difficult to interact with other people. During one of her combined treatment sessions, she gave him a danburite crystal (right) and told him he could mix with anyone. Unfortunately, she did not realize that in some social groups to "mix it" or to "mix it up" means to fight and argue. Which he did! Every time he met someone new!

CHILDREN

Jade is traditionally one of the first stones to give a child as it protects them in the great adventure playground called life.

The demands of children can sometimes be a challenge. Whether you feel this way with all children, some children, or one child in particular, mookaite is the crystal to turn to, to make it easier for you to cope.

All children develop differently, and some have special abilities noticeable from a young age. They are sometimes called "indigo" or "crystal" children, and sugilite can help them develop their gifts.

Mookaite can help you cope with the demands of young adventurers.

Allow children to explore the magic of crystals from an early age.

LIVING WITH OTHERS

It is a natural human trait to wish to comprehend others, whether it is those speaking foreign languages or even other species. People who spend a lot of time around animals begin to understand their nature and often even "hear" what they are saying through sound, action, and body language. Abalone shell's shimmering shades can help you translate animal talk into meaning that you understand. It works both ways and will also help animals to understand you.

For any external disturbances, such as noisy neighbors or traffic, place pyrite on each of your window ledges. Your life will become almost instantly quieter (see box, below).

Abalone shell will improve your communication with pets and other animals in your life.

The power of pyrite

The first time I discovered the power of pyrite, I was teaching a meditation class in a town-center location. It was a hot summer's night and the windows were wide open when a noisy commotion broke out on the street outside. A large pyrite crystal called to me, and not really knowing what I was doing or why, I placed it on the window ledge. The noise instantly stopped, as if I had closed the window. I turned to the room to see the look of shock and surprise on every student's face!

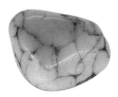

Career and study

Richness in life can take different forms for different people. Finding your purpose and exploring new ways to flourish and grow is important for the well-being of many, whether this is linked to work or career, new adventures or projects in the home, or building knowledge for the future.

Crystals for fulfillment include (from top) amber, dalmation stone, howlite, and vanadinite.

Abundance might include money and wealth, but can also include health, knowledge, wisdom, kindness, honesty, morality, and more. Amber, dalmatian stone, howlite, jade, jasper, and vanadinite can all be helpful in your quest for a more fulfilled lifestyle.

Ruby will help you focus on abundance from your heart, helping you not only to accumulate everything you need in life, but to share this profusion with others too. If you have an abundance of wealth, ruby will also keep you financially focused on what is realistic and feasible.

Garnet energizes activities which bring abundance, including physical work, deep intellectual challenge, and study that will bring increased future income. Amethyst brings your own spirituality into your business and promotes success.

If you are completely addicted to the material world and would like to change your lifestyle, then try working with lepidolite to shift your behavior patterns and to let it float away. (See also Addiction, page 91.)

Lepidolite will help you break away from patterns of behavior that are no longer serving you.

DREAMS, DESIRES, AND AMBITION

When you follow your life path, magical things seem to just happen around you. When you stray off the path, you discover obstacles that become increasingly insurmountable the farther you drift (see also Flow, page 76). Wear sapphire or labradorite to help your ambitions manifest.

We unconsciously manifest our desires and plot our successes in our nighttime dreams. How often do we absolutely know that we have found an answer in our dreams and yet can't quite remember it in the morning? Celestite, amethyst, and lapis lazuli can all enhance the dream state and promote dream recall.

For some people, desires, dreams, goals, and ideas can be inspiring and an amazing driving force that powers your dreams to fulfillment. However, ambition can also disrupt your true life's purpose. For some, ambition can become obsessive to the point of being debilitating, and sapphire will help you to control your desires if they are becoming compulsive. It will help you to find balance, bringing realism to the overly ambitious and drive and direction to those who need it. The key word here is "need" not "want"—kunzite brings desire to the surface, allowing you to consider whether it is really something you want to pursue or not.

Many forms of motivation may be for the benefit of others as well as oneself, but for some people, personal ambition is a powerful motivator. Personal ambition is precisely that—completely about yourself. Surround yourself with bowenite to stay focused. I would also temper it with sapphire to avoid burnout.

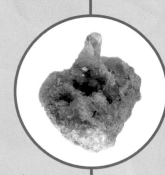

Sleep with celestite (right) to promote dreaming and to help you remember your dreams when you wake up.

Citrine (top) is a money magnet that attracts financial success to any endeavor, while tiger's eye (center) and jet (bottom) bring the energy needed for those starting out in business or long-term projects.

MONEY AND WEALTH

Citrine, known as the "money stone," is like a money magnet—it attracts wealth. Keep a citrine crystal with you in your pocket, purse, or wallet at all times. Place one by the entrance to your place of work, whether that is a store, factory, warehouse, or the cab of your work vehicle. Business owners should keep one in their cash register, in a drawer or file where bank information is kept, next to your computer if you have an online business, or if you take orders or appointments over the phone, with your telephone. In fact, wherever your income comes from is a wonderful place to keep a citrine crystal!

Tiger's eye is a wonderful asset when you are starting a business as it will give new financial projects a kick start, while jet is a slow-burning aid that is recommended for longer-term projects.

Stibnite is good for fiscal planning and management, helping you keep track of day-to-day expenditure, while sunstone illuminates opportunities and tektite brings abundance from unexpected sources. Once you have acquired your money, turn to tourmaline to protect your assets—the green variety is best for this.

MANAGEMENT SKILLS

Management can be related to work situations, but it can also be about managing any situation in any area of your life, whether it involves others or not. It is how we help others and ourselves cope.

Morganite is a helpful crystal, which promotes time management and will help you to organize your time effectively. Lapis lazuli and fluorite can also help. The former aids organizational skills while the latter brings order to chaos.

Negotiation is all about agreement. A deal is only a deal if everyone is happy with it, otherwise it is an arrangement that someone does not like. Amethyst and tourmaline ease these situations and can help you succeed.

Manage your time and your money effectively with stibnite (top) and morganite (above).

LEADERSHIP

Leadership in any field can be enhanced by aventurine and pyrite. Fluorite can also help to get everyone focusing on the same goals and sodalite will bring minds onto the same wavelength, while tourmaline and yellow fluorite promote teamwork.

LEARNING AND EXAMS

If you are studying for exams, then amazonite, aventurine, fluorite, and snow quartz work very well together. Amazonite calms the nerves and aventurine relaxes the muscles. Should your concentration waiver for any reason, snow quartz clears the mind from distractions and fluorite focuses it on your study.

Study aids

Whether you are studying for a qualification or out of pure joy and personal interest, there are several crystals that can help in the pursuit of knowledge. Aquamarine (top), calcite (center), carnelian, citrine, dalmatian stone (bottom), howlite, lepidolite, obsidian, purple fluorite, ruby, and snow quartz all work well.

Emotional well-being

On the following pages, I want to focus on the mind and how it can affect your everyday life.

There are all sorts of reasons as to why we might sometimes have to stop or slow down. Physical illness or injury can do that to you and I have covered health and healing extensively in other books (see Resources, page 137). Some physical issues, such as stamina, sleep, and weight management, can affect your overall well-being, and there are crystals that can help. If you have an issue with physical activity, try holding or wearing rutilated quartz while getting up and moving around—it will give you a lift and get your motor running again. The go-to crystal to aid a good night's sleep and a regular sleep pattern is malachite (see also Bedrooms, page 37). Apatite is a tiny piece of magic for those who find it difficult to control their diet in our 21st-century world. Whenever there are emotional reasons for weight fluctuation, simply hold an apatite crystal for 120 seconds before you eat anything, whether a snack or a five-course meal. If you still feel you need to eat, then do. You will quickly find that you just do not eat as much, or if you need to put on weight, you begin to eat more. Whether your need is physical, emotional, mental, or spiritual, smoky quartz can bring yang energy to anything you are doing that needs a bit more "muscle."

MENTAL HEALTH AND WELL-BEING

The balance between the left and right hemispheres of your brain is vital to your welfare and happiness. This is the place where intellect meets intuition, and science and magic converge.

Wearing rutilated quartz can help to get you moving

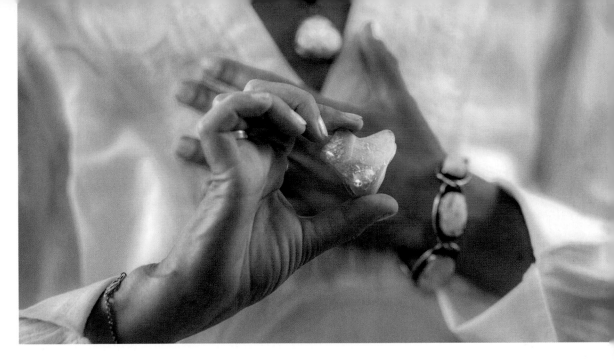

Chalcopyrite, labradorite, and tourmaline all aid a state of equilibrium. They each bring magic into your life in diverse ways. Chalcopyrite helps you notice the world around you and see opportunities in different and wondrous ways. Labradorite eases the flow of energy around you, so it feels that magic just happens around you wherever you are. And tourmaline gives you a sense of protection, offering you the freedom to explore in any way you wish.

Sometimes you can feel stuck, as if you are in a rut and just cannot get yourself out, which can lead to mental and emotional stagnation and depression. In extreme cases it can even stop you from functioning. Aventurine can motivate you to get moving again. When your brain just seems to stop, as if it has suddenly frozen and you cannot even think or remember what it is you are trying to do, then hold a ruby crystal to kick-start your mind into motion. And for times it feels like there is a fog in your head you cannot see through, hold chrysoprase to clear the mists so you can see clearly what you need to do.

Aventurine offers motivation when you feel you cannot move forward.

Labradorite (above right) and chalcopyrite (right) offer balance and equilibrium.

Green calcite (top) and fire agate (above) can help you to manage the effects of stress and anxiety.

STRESS AND ANXIETY

Quite simply, as human beings, we are not designed to live in the 21st-century world we have created. We are exasperated by running around, with too many people in too small an area, trying to do too much, and being in too many places at once. This results in our fight-or-flight response being kicked off continuously (see box, opposite). The combined effects of rhodochrosite and rhodonite can get to the source of your troubles.

Anxiety can be disempowering, and panic attacks can be completely disabling. Carry green calcite with you and hold it at the first signs of nervousness or unease. In extreme situations, stress and anxiety can cause complete burnout. Fire agate can reenergize you and start to get you back on track.

Sometimes when we are stressed, worried, or concerned about someone or something, we can easily lose our perspective. Tourmaline will help you see the funny side of situations and refresh your outlook on life in general.

TRAUMA

For any type of traumatic experience, hold an aqua aura crystal. Within a few minutes, your body and mind will start to calm. Years ago, I witnessed an accident outside my store and heard this crystal call to me. A moment later, a lady walked into the store covered in blood. It was not her blood; she had been helping someone who was severely injured in the accident and was now in shock. I was amazed at how quick and effective this magical crystal was in bringing relief and a sense of being able to function to her once again.

Aqua aura can help you cope with traumatic situations.

Fight or flight

The fight-or-flight response is a magical, internal, biochemical reaction designed to keep us alive. It is designed so that thousands of years ago, when you are out collecting roots and berries and a saber tooth tiger appears, a survival response is triggered. Your body instantly produces 200 natural biochemicals, which change you from a kind, loving person into one of the most violent, vicious animals on the planet. In fact, we have come to dominate the planet because this survival mechanism is the best evolution can buy.

The fight-or-flight response is the only natural reaction we have to any type of perceived threat. It is not designed for the 21st-century lifestyle. So, if your boss says something that you do not like, you have only two possible responses: you can punch them on the nose or run away. Neither are illustrious career moves! If we do neither we become stressed.

We also have a natural relaxation response. This produces another 198 chemicals in your body and re-sets you back to being a loving, kind person. This is not instantaneous and takes about 15 minutes. In our 21st-century lifestyle our relaxation response is more often than not interrupted, and you are left with all these chemicals in your system that change your feelings and behavior, which causes stress.

GRIEF AND LOSS

The longer you live, the more likely it is that you will be affected by heartache in one form or another. Grief—for example, from the loss of a relative, friend, or pet—is a big influence in our lives. The go-to crystal for any loss is smoky quartz, which helps to alleviate grief and release suppressed tears.

I also want to consider that many (but by no means all) grief is really linked to the loss of an ideal and not a reality. This is often the truth with situations such as the ending of a marriage or relationship or a job or career. The grief is not really for the loss of the person or situation, it is more likely to be for what you hoped it would be. It is the loss of the dream. In this situation turn to unakite to support you. It brings an instant "hug" and longer-term healing as you come to terms with this very different kind of loss. It will allow you to let go of the past, move forward, and enjoy your new reality.

Other types of loss, such as moving home, can be made easier with crystals. The experience of moving is made easier with bowenite. If you are emigrating, petrified wood can help you leave the past behind, making it easier for you to start your new life.

Crystals such as (from top) smoky quartz, obsidian, and unakite can support you through the many kinds of grief in our lives.

Bowenite can make the experience of moving home easier.

ADDICTION

Kunzite is the go-to crystal for any type of addiction, whether behavioural or chemical. Whatever habit you want to change in your life, simply keep a kunzite crystal with you 24/7. Whenever you feel a craving, hold the crystal for two minutes—really, 120 seconds, that's all—before you act on it. You will find that this immediately cuts out about 50 percent of your dependence. Persevere for a few weeks and you will notice that your dependence will have greatly reduced, or completely vanished as if they had never been.

Carrying lepidolite or charoite with you can also help to break cycles and behavior patterns you keep repeating. Kunzite is particularly good for smoking cessation, amethyst can help especially with issues around alcohol, and peridot with compulsive eating.

It is known that many addictive behaviors can stem from childhood experiences, so it will be worthwhile adding blue chalcedony to your addiction crystal medicine bag.

DEALING WITH LIFE'S MISHAPS

Accidents happen. Whether you could have prevented it, altered it, caused it, or it just happened, that's life. Sometimes the Universe can appear to be quite unfair, as if it has deliberately picked you out for some devious purpose of its own.

If mishaps keep happening around you, then carry or wear jade. It brings balance and evens out the fates that the Universe appears to be throwing at you. Tourmaline can help, too, and will protect you if you are feeling accident-prone. If your property is affected by misfortune, then turquoise will help to keep it safe.

As a final tip, it could be worth carrying or wearing pyrite. This crystal can function as a spark that will kick you into action just before an accident, thereby preventing it from ever happening in the first place.

Jade offers balance through life's mishaps, no matter what the Universe seems to throw at you.

Spiritual well-being

Speaking your truth and living your life in your own spiritual way is healthy and liberating in so many ways. Aquamarine, kyanite, and turquoise will all help you express your truth.

Magic happens all the time, every day, all day. Mostly we just do not recognize it when it happens. Like the Roald Dahl adage, "Those who don't believe in magic will never find it." Being connected to our surroundings, nature, the environment, and being aware of the magic in everything is good for the spirit. Labradorite is great for this—with its beautiful labradorescence of colors, it will illuminate the magical.

Connect to your surroundings with labradorite (above) and become aware of the magic all around you.

CONNECTING WITH THE WORLD

First Nations Peoples of North America believe that a journey is always spiritual, whether you are walking to the local store, taking a trip round the world, or following your path through life. Whatever journey you are currently on or planning, turquoise will keep you safe. Aquamarine is perfect for mariners, or for any water travel, such as a cruise or yacht trip, or for water sports like surfing or swimming. (See also Traveling for Work, page 65.)

Sometimes, you may feel a deep desire to travel for no clear reason, but moonstone will help you understand why your soul feels the need to roam or explore.

Tourmaline enhances your connection to nature and is a great crystal to work with if you want to save the planet. Septarian increases your awareness of green issues. Chrysocolla also promotes the desire to heal the Earth, and also the effectiveness of Earth healing.

Sometimes, we take time out of our usual world—either through choice, such as a trip or a retreat, or perhaps enforced, due to illness or incarceration. Danburite will help you to re-enter the world after you have been away for any reason.

Turquoise (top) and aquamarine (above) will protect you on life's journey.

CONNECTING TO THE DIVINE

We all have moments when we wish we could find a little guidance from another plane. Divine energy—whether you choose to call this God, Goddess, Great Spirit, Jesus, Krishna, Buddha, Mohammed, angels, spirit guides, ancestors, the Universe, or anything else—is all around us all the time. It is happy and willing to help if we ask. Lemurian quartz crystal, petrified wood, amethyst, celestite, angel aura quartz, and aqua aura can all help you connect to this divine energy.

Connect to the divine with angel aura quartz.

Chapter 5

The Crystal Finder

101 crystals and their lifestyle benefits 96

Red 100

Orange 102

Yellow 104

Green 107

Pink 111

Multicolor and
rainbow 114

Blue 118

Violet 123

White and clear 126

Black 130

Silver and gray 132

Brown 134

101 crystals and their lifestyle benefits

On the following pages you will find 101 crystals that can help you on your journey through life.

The crystals are arranged by color to help you identify the ones you already have or may come across in the future. Each one is listed in its most commonly available color. Many crystals naturally form in several colors, and these are also noted in the descriptions, alongside photographs to aid recognition. The crystal formations are also described—see also the Glossary (page 138), which explains some of the terms used to describe crystal forms. You can use the color sections, photographs, and descriptions to identify each crystal by its color and formation.

The common sources listed give the naturally occurring locations of the crystals that you may find in your local crystal store. Except where there is only one source listed, most minerals have many sources around the world and local sources may vary significantly.

To inspire you to explore some of the possibilities that the mineral kingdom has to offer, each crystal is also listed with its astrological associations, the chakra connected to each one, and a description of their lifestyle qualities. This information will assist you in choosing crystals you are drawn to, or that may help in the plethora of situations you encounter on your life journey. If you are searching for a crystal to help with a specific issue, open your mind to alternative words that might describe the same or a similar topic, because there just isn't room to list every possible descriptive word for related themes.

I have covered the physical healing attributes of these crystals in other books (see Resources, page 137), which cover this aspect of crystals in detail, and you might find helpful.

Opposite: Identify the crystals you already have, or may come across in the future, by their color and formation.

Dowsing with a crystal pendulum

We all have an inner pendulum. It is the natural mechanism that guides you safely through life. Everyone is aware of their inner pendulum some of the time, but usually only in extreme moments of joy or stress.

We've all experienced these moments—that feeling that rises through your body, lifts you up, and shouts, "Wow! This is amazing!" when you experience something marvelous and that sinking feeling when your stomach seems to fall through your body to the floor and says, "Get me out of here NOW!"

Your inner pendulum is working all the time. Small, subtle, internal movements say "yes" or "no" to everything you do, everyone you meet, everywhere you go, what you watch, listen to—even as you are reading this book.

When you work with a crystal pendulum, it is showing you an external, physical representation of what your inner pendulum is doing inside you, making it even easier and quicker for you to tap into your natural response or intuition. The more you work with your crystal pendulum, the more you will recognize your inner pendulum.

Dowsing is an ancient and natural human ability – it is one of the oldest forms of divination (see Resources, page 137). Dowsing rods, or forked twigs, can be used to answer any question you wish to ask, but many people find a pendulum is the easiest dowsing tool to work with.

1 Hold the pendulum by the top of the chain or bead.
2 Ask the pendulum to show you a "yes."
3 Be patient. The pendulum will move in one of four ways: back and forth, side to side, clockwise, or counterclockwise. Don't worry if it is a very small movement; it will get bigger as you

Your pendulum will tap into your natural intuition and help you to choose the crystals that are right for you.

continue to work with your crystal pendulum. Note the direction your pendulum moves in. If it fails to move, hold a hematite crystal in your other hand to help you ground.

4   Ask the pendulum to show you a "no." You will see one of the four possible movements, different to the movement you received in step 3. Again, note the direction your pendulum moves in.

5   Now you know what your pendulum's "yes" and "no" look like. Your pendulum can help you select crystals that are right for you. Simply hold the pendulum over a crystal, ask whether it is the right choice for you, and observe the pendulum's movement.

Red

Red crystals give you the courage to take the next step on your journey—whether physical, emotional, mental, or spiritual—so you can move forward in your life.

RED JASPER

This stone is a massive variety of quartz, which is colored red due to inclusions of iron oxide.

Common source: Brazil and India.

Astrological associations: Taurus and Aries.

Chakra: Base.

Lifestyle qualities: Red jasper is connected to rebirth of all kinds, from fresh starts to new ideas. It stimulates survival instincts, is a mood elevator, and promotes fulfillment. It is also a grounding crystal, which supports the immune system (keeping you well when mixing with others) and aids sleep (especially against physical disturbances).

RED CALCITE

This crystal is a pale to deep red variety of calcite found in the form of rock masses.

Common source: Mexico.

Astrological associations: Cancer.

Chakra: Base.

Lifestyle qualities: A calming, grounding, and feel-good crystal that offers emotional protection and sacred connection. Red calcite is good for ADHD (attention deficit hyperactivity disorder), panic attacks, anxiety, and OCD (obsessive compulsive disorder). It also promotes learning.

MOOKAITE

A patterned, red-and-cream variety of jasper.

Common source: Australia.

Astrological associations: Leo.

Chakra: Base.

Lifestyle qualities: Mookaite is a calming, grounding stone that helps life to flow better, allowing you to move forward. Good for coping with children and communication, it helps you speak kindly in difficult situations. It boosts protection and self-esteem and dispels fear, depression, and loneliness. This crystal can alter your perceptions, leading to creative solutions and new ideas and influencing any decisions you might be making. Good for dreams, job seeking, weight loss, and meditation.

GARNET

Garnet is found as dodecahedral and trapezohedral crystals and combinations, masses, and layered "plates." Its forms include red, pink eudialyte, pink/red rhodolite, green grossularite, emerald green uvarovite, black melanite, orange spessartine, red/purple almandine, greenish yellow andradite, yellow and brown hessonite.

Common source: India, Russia, and USA.

Astrological associations: Leo, Virgo, Capricorn, and Aquarius.

Chakra: Heart.

Lifestyle qualities: This crystal boosts numeracy and awareness, linking the left and right sides of the brain so you can consider problems from different angles. It can reduce chaos in your life by making big life changes flow more easily, relieving emotional trauma, balancing emotions, and easing depression. Garnet is connected with vitality, courage, and abundance, and is good for physical work or study. It is a magical crystal and promotes spiritual practices such as meditation and yoga.

BRECCIATED JASPER

Brecciated jasper is formed when jasper is shattered by tectonic activity. During this process, the spaces created are filled with more jasper, chalcedony, and different varieties of macrocrystalline quartz. The deep red colors are due to hematite (see page 133) embedded within the jasper.

Common source: Worldwide, including Australia, Brazil, Canada, Egypt, Madagascar, India, Russia, Republic of South Africa, USA, and Uruguay.

Astrological associations: Taurus and Aries.

Chakra: Base.

Lifestyle qualities: Brecciated jasper is associated with rebuilding and is a wonderful crystal for putting your life back together after a trauma, disaster, or calamity on any level. It can help to lift your mood, promote fertility, and alleviate addiction. Brecciated jasper is a grounding crystal and is good for bringing people together into a team as it helps with unifying different ideas and seeing different viewpoints.

RUBY

Ruby is the red variety of corundum, which forms tabular crystals.

Common source: India, Madagascar, Thailand, and Myanmar.

Astrological associations: Leo, Scorpio, Cancer and Sagittarius.

Chakra: Heart.

Lifestyle qualities: Associated with knowledge and self-cultivation, ruby will kick your mind into gear when you feel stuck. It will help you with new beginnings, creativity, making decisions or changes, financial realism, and finding answers to questions about love and relationships. It brings abundance and helps you share it from your heart. This crystal protects from nightmares, relieves anguish, distress, and suffering, helps with distant healing, and strengthens connections with spirit guides.

Orange

Orange crystals bring the vibrant energy of the Sun into your life. They can pick you up when you're feeling down and help to inspire creativity within and around you.

ORANGE CALCITE

Orange calcite forms in rock masses and is found in bright to pale orange hues.

Common source: Mexico.

Astrological associations: Cancer and Leo.

Chakra: Sacral.

Lifestyle qualities: This crystal will help you to laugh and smile at life's foibles. It will bring balance to your energy by physically calming when you're feeling stressed and imbuing you with a sense of vitality when you are following your destiny. Orange calcite can inspire your creative abilities.

VANADINITE

Vanadinite is found in the form of barrel-shaped or hollow, prismatic crystals and masses.

Common source: Morocco.

Astrological associations: Virgo.

Chakra: Sacral.

Lifestyle qualities: Vanadinite brings the possibility of a fulfilled lifestyle. While some people might try to "buy" their dreams, vanadinite will allow you to calculate better approaches toward your goals in life by promoting your thought processes and mental abilities. It boosts fame and reputation while helping to relieve exhaustion. It can also aid meditation.

CAUTION: Not suitable as an elixir.

HALITE

Halite forms massive or cubic salt crystals and may be clear, orange, yellow, red, blue, pink, green, or multicolored.

Common source: Pakistan (orange), USA (pink and red), Germany (blue), and Australia (green).

Astrological associations: Cancer and Pisces.

Chakra: Sacral.

Lifestyle qualities: Halite can bring balance to your energy and help to ease mood swings. This in turn can give you more stamina to deal with troublesome situations that affect your personality.

CAUTION: Not suitable as an elixir.

CARNELIAN

Carnelian is a variety of chalcedony, which commonly forms as pebbles. The stones are primarily orange but can also be found in red, pink, or brown hues.
Common source: Brazil, India, and Uruguay.
Astrological associations: Taurus, Cancer, and Leo.
Chakra: Sacral.
Lifestyle qualities: Carnelian can help with infections, so will help you keep going when you're feeling physically down. It will not only give you vitality and energy in physical situations, but also boost courage, self-esteem, and confidence. Carnelian will help anyone experiencing memory or apathy problems while studying as it frees your mind and helps with focus and expression of creative ideas. For performers, or anyone needing to speak, sing, or shout out, this crystal is great for the voice and helps to boost fame or reputation.

SUNSTONE

A type of oligoclase, sunstone is a variety of the feldspar mineral plagioclase. Goethite and hematite are common inclusions, which give this crystal its sparkly appearance.
Common source: India.
Astrological associations: Leo and Libra.
Chakra: Crown.
Lifestyle qualities: Sunstone is associated with vitality leading to longevity. It illuminates opportunities, which will help you to create abundance and brings physical strength and energy to help you overcome fear and the stress associated with anxiety.

Yellow

Yellow crystals stimulate creative energy and courage.
They bring abundance in all fields.

GOLDEN HEALER QUARTZ

Quartz crystals with yellow iron that is included within, or coats the crystal (either partially or fully).
Common source: Worldwide.
Astrological associations: All.
Chakra: All, especially Heart.
Lifestyle qualities: Golden healer quartz helps you to recognize your inner self and find satisfaction within. It can ease, shift, and facilitate emotional health and healing and remove the unhealthy blocks that are preventing you from changing your behavior patterns or making lifestyle changes. It will help you to cut ties with the past and release fear, hurt, and self-judgmental thoughts. It brings emotional balance, restoring your self-esteem after disappointment. This crystal can also heal rooms that hold traumatic energy. Golden healer quartz is a happy crystal that attracts abundance and prosperity, relationships, and will help you to "walk your walk" through life.

TIGER'S EYE

Tiger's eye occurs when quartz replaces asbestos and forms a chatoyancy effect due to the previous fibrous asbestos structure. (Note, however, that there is no asbestos present in tiger's eye.) Tiger's eye is a gold/yellow/brown color, or can occur as a blue hawk's eye or red falcon's eye.
Common source: Republic of South Africa.
Astrological associations: Capricorn.
Chakra: Solar Plexus.
Lifestyle qualities: A stone that inspires a "just do it" attitude, tiger's eye can give you a kickstart, or an extra bit of muscle when you need physical strength and stamina. It sharpens the mind and fosters mental balance between the right and left sides of the brain and the female and male energies within you. Tiger's eye discourages turmoil and negativity (from fear, worry, inhibition, and introversion to depression, narrow mindedness, and stubbornness) and is grounding, encouraging calm, intuition, creativity, and courage. This crystal brings choices, new beginnings, luck, wealth, and prosperity. Tiger's eye will make you feel better and can help with any form of distant healing. The red variety promotes sexuality.

CITRINE

Yellow, golden, or lemon variety of quartz, color is due to heat from volcanic and other earth activity.
Common source: Brazil and Democratic Republic of Congo.
Astrological associations: Gemini, Aries, Libra, and Leo.
Chakra: Solar Plexus.
Lifestyle qualities: Citrine balances the female and male energies within you, boosting your aura, awareness, self-esteem, and confidence, and making you feel better. Citrine attracts abundance. Not only does it act as a money magnet, bringing wealth and prosperity, but also joy, happiness, creativity, and success. It promotes new beginnings, healthy and loving relationships, and making wise choices, and is linked to teaching and studying (learning), promoting writing and problem solving. It helps to alleviate stress and releases emotional toxins, such as anger and jealousy.

AMBER

Amber is the fossilized resin from prehistoric trees. It sometimes has inclusions of animal and/or plant material and can be found in yellow, orange, brown, and blue colors, or in an artificial, green color.
Common source: Baltic Sea region (including Poland, Lithuania, and Latvia).
Astrological associations: Leo and Aquarius.
Chakra: Solar Plexus.
Lifestyle qualities: Amber aids memory. It helps you to learn from past experiences and releases negativity and emotional blockages, leaving you free to fulfill your dreams, goals, and ideals. It's good for making intellectual choices. Calming amber balances female and male energies within you, brings good luck and protection, and symbolizes renewal of marriage vows (like an eternity ring). Amber purifies body, mind, and spirit. It can be burned as an incense to cleanse and remove negativity from a room or space. As an elixir, it is a magical cure for constipation.

COPPER

Copper is a metal forming free-form shapes, dendrites, plates, and rhombohedral crystals.
Common source: North, South, and Central America—USA, and Chile.
Astrological associations: Taurus and Sagittarius.
Chakra: Sacral.
Lifestyle qualities: Copper brings emotional balance. It energizes, revitalizes, and generally makes you feel better. Copper crystals promote fame and reputation and liberate sexuality.
CAUTION: Not suitable as an elixir.

YELLOW FLUORITE

Yellow fluorite forms cubic, octahedral, and rhombododecahedral crystals and masses in yellow hues.
Common source: China and UK.
Astrological associations: Leo.
Chakra: Sacral.
Lifestyle qualities: Yellow fluorite brings order out of chaos. It is connected to a healthy mind, promoting thought, focus, creativity, and ideas, which will help you reach your goals. This crystal enables healthy, loving relationships and teamwork. Yellow fluorite can also help with weight loss and alleviates the effect of too much screen time.

GOLDEN CALCITE

Golden calcite takes the form of bright, golden-colored, rhombohedral crystals.
Common source: China.
Astrological associations: Leo and Cancer.
Chakra: Solar Plexus.
Lifestyle qualities: This crystal offers sacred connection and emotional protection, calming the nerves, promoting feelings of security and safety, and allowing you to ditch self-limiting beliefs. Golden calcite generates positivity and feel-good feelings. It's good for study, past-life recall, calm communication, creativity, and inspiration.

Green

Green crystals bring emotions to the fore and promote serenity, health, healing, and wisdom.

AVENTURINE

A variety of quartz, aventurine has inclusions of mica that give this crystal a speckled or sparkly effect. Commonly green, aventurine can also be found in blue, white, red/peach, and brown hues.

Common source: Brazil and India.
Astrological associations: Aries.
Chakra: Heart.
Lifestyle qualities: Aventurine brings motivation, inspiration, creativity, and success. It is also a relaxing crystal that calms the mind and soothes emotions, and so is perfect for pre-exam and exam stress. It will balance your female and male aspects. Aventurine will connect you to spirit guides and is good for leadership and decision-making. This protective stone will also guard against "energy vampires."

MALACHITE

Malachite is green, often with various shades of green and black bands. Formed as crystalline aggregates, druses, botryoidal structures, and clusters of radiating fibrous crystals, single prismatic crystals of malachite are rare. More common are malachite pseudomorphs of azurite, which produce a more tabby crystal.

Common source: Democratic Republic of Congo and USA.
Astrological associations: Capricorn and Scorpio.
Chakra: Heart.
Lifestyle qualities: Malachite links us to our ancestors and the past. It is very calming, helping to release big emotions, dispelling depression and insomnia, and promoting restful sleep, healthy sleep patterns, and dream interpretation. It also aids the heart connection in meditation.
CAUTION: Not suitable as an elixir.

AMAZONITE

Amazonite is a green, usually opaque, variety of microcline (a variety of feldspar). Its color can vary, from yellow-green to blue-green, and it forms crystals and masses.

Common source: Brazil, Russia, and USA.
Astrological associations: Virgo.
Chakra: Heart.
Lifestyle qualities: This calming crystal will soothe nervousness and a troubled mind, reducing stress and making you feel good. Amazonite allows your creativity to flow.

UNAKITE

Unakite is a mixture of epidote, feldspar, and quartz in massive rock form.

Common source: Republic of South Africa.

Astrological associations: Scorpio.

Chakra: Heart.

Lifestyle qualities: Unakite will help you cope with grief, both the sorrow associated with the loss of a loved one, but especially with the loss of an idea or concept, dream, or goal. It helps you to learn from past experiences and lives, so you can see and move past blocks you put in your own way. This crystal connects the Base and Heart chakras, keeping you in the present moment and allowing you to move forward from your heart. Unakite is calming for the emotions and balances the female and male energy within.

CHRYSOCOLLA

Chrysocolla forms in layers, masses, botryoidal structures, and druses.

Common source: Peru and USA.

Astrological associations: Gemini, Virgo, and Taurus.

Chakra: Heart.

Lifestyle qualities: Chrysocolla will help you to recognize emotional and behavioral cycles, so you can focus on those that are helpful and let go of the harmful ones. This crystal relieves tension from stressful situations and releases negative emotions, such as phobias, guilt, and emotional heartache. (Chrysocolla will help to heal a broken heart.) This crystal will help you to feel good and releases your innate creativity. It boosts sexuality, revitalizing relationships. It is good for Earth healing—chrysocolla spheres even look like planets!

JADE

Jade occurs in massive forms and in many colors, including green, orange, brown, blue, cream, white, lavender, red, gray, and black. Different types of jade include jadeite and nephrite. New jade is actually bowenite (see page 110).

Common source: Canada, China, Myanmar, and USA.

Astrological associations: Aries, Gemini, Taurus, and Libra.

Chakra: Heart.

Lifestyle qualities: Jade is connected to spirit and the knowledge of ancient civilizations, making it a perfect stone for problem solving, self-cultivation, and fulfillment. Jade is the first stone traditionally offered to a child, as it offers protection from negativity and accidents, as well as wisdom and longevity. It also promotes dreams and dream recall. Filled with modesty and compassion it brings justice to most situations and offers courage and confidence. It is a stone of emotional balance, bringing inner and outer peace.

GREEN CALCITE

Green calcite forms as massive rocks.
Common source: Mexico.
Astrological associations: Cancer.
Chakra: Heart.
Lifestyle qualities: Green calcite protects your emotions, reducing anxiety, worry, and panic attacks, helping you to feel good. It is the best thing to keep you calm during big life changes and as you learn from experience.

EMERALD

Emerald is the green gem variety of beryl.
Common source: Columbia (for gem quality) and Brazil (for commercial grade).
Astrological associations: Taurus, Gemini, and Aries.
Chakra: Heart.
Lifestyle qualities: Emerald promotes memory and offers love, honesty, and patience, which aids relationships and marriage.

CHRYSOPRASE

Chrysoprase is a green or yellow (lemon chrysoprase) variety of chalcedony.
Common source: Australia.
Astrological associations: Libra.
Chakra: Heart.
Lifestyle qualities: Chrysoprase helps you see through the confusion in your mind. It clears the fog that holds anxiety, depression, fear, inhibitions, neurotic patterns, arrogance, and judgmental attitudes so you can find and accept the root cause of your stress. This crystal promotes meditation and brings mental health and healing. It will help you to achieve a balanced acceptance of both others and yourself, leaving you happy and feeling good.

FUCHSITE

Fuchsite is variety of mica. Its chromium inclusions give this crystal its green color. It forms platy layers, masses, and occasionally as tabular crystals.
Common source: Brazil.
Astrological associations: Aquarius.
Chakra: Heart.
Lifestyle qualities: This calming crystal is good for emotional recovery, such as from unrequited love or trauma. It is also good for calming skin conditions exacerbated

by stress, such as eczema and psoriasis. Fuchsite allows energy to flow and helps you make the right choices.
CAUTION: Not suitable as an elixir.

PERIDOT

Peridot forms small, prismatic crystals and masses. It is primarily green but other colors include red, brown, and yellow.

Common source: Afghanistan, Brazil, Canary Islands, Pakistan, Russia, Sri Lanka, and USA.

Astrological associations: Virgo, Leo, Scorpio, and Sagittarius.

Chakra: Heart.

Lifestyle qualities: Peridot is a feel-good crystal in every way. It promotes the digestion of new ideas and brings enlightenment through meditation, personal growth, and development. It releases emotional blockages caused by past stress and will help you to let go of unhealthy behavior patterns and cycles, from compulsive eating and addiction, to depression, lethargy, and laziness, to egoism, anger, and jealousy. Peridot also offers protection from outside influences, providing space for your mental health and healing.

BOWENITE

Bowenite is a green variety of antigorite, forming massive, fine, granular rock.

Common source: China and USA.

Astrological associations: Aquarius.

Chakra: Heart.

Lifestyle qualities: Bowenite is known as the "stone of the warrior." It will protect you from enemies, and from unkind thoughts and words. It removes blocks that are put in your way, either by yourself or others, helping you to stop being a sheep, to follow your own path rather than that of others, overcome fear of success, and start to make positive changes in your life. Bowenite promotes personal ambition, self-reliance, and focus on your inner self. It will make your adventures—in all fields, from business to personal goals and ambitions—so much more fun.

Bowenite helps you make a "clean break" from the past. It helps you cope with emotional stresses, such as grief, and move beyond previous trauma, leaving you with the freedom to travel your path, make changes, and embark on new adventures. It's a good stone to have when moving home.

This crystal promotes love and friendship and will help you to discover your soul mate. It connects you to your ancestors, aiding meditation to find answers and insight.

BLOODSTONE

Bloodstone is a form of green jasper, often with red inclusions. With the red inclusions it is known as heliotrope bloodstone and with little or no red flecks, it is known as plasma bloodstone.

Common source: India.

Astrological associations: Aries, Pisces, and Libra.

Chakra: Heart.

Lifestyle qualities: Bloodstone is calming and emotionally centering, aiding courage, vitality, and

creativity. It will soothe disproportionate stress caused by cuts, bruises, and other minor injuries, and is also good for controlling a bad temper through gentle release.

Pink

Pink crystals warm the heart and soothe the soul.
They carry powerful love and gentle compassion.

MORGANITE

Morganite is a variety of beryl that forms as pink, hexagonal crystals.
Common source: Brazil and Pakistan.
Astrological associations: Libra.
Chakra: Heart.
Lifestyle qualities: Morganite will encourage you to see the inner beauty of those you meet. It is connected with love and marriage and can help to repair relationships. This crystal fills the space left in the heart by grief, whether from a broken relationship or from the loss of a loved one. A good crystal for ceremonies, morganite calms the mind, aids meditation, and promotes contact with spirit guides. Morganite brings clear thought, promoting wisdom, the ability to see things from a different perspective, the eradication of bigotry (such as racism and sexism), and improved time management. It helps you to take the initiative and bring ideas to the table.

COBALTOAN CALCITE

Cobaltoan calcite forms drusy crusts, spherical masses and rare crystals often associated with malachite.
Common source: Democratic Republic of Congo and Morocco.
Astrological associations: Cancer.
Chakra: Heart, Throat, Brow, and Crown.
Lifestyle qualities: Cobaltoan calcite helps you to see the beauty in everyone, everything, and every situation you encounter. With this crystal, you will recognize and learn each lesson along your path with gratitude, inner truth, and life purpose. It is calming, protecting your emotions and supporting emotional expression and allowing you to draw out inner hurts and emotional pain. This feel-good crystal will attract your desires.

ROSE QUARTZ

Rose quartz forms as pink, crystalline masses and occasionally as rare, small, hexagonal crystals.
Common source: Brazil, India, Madagascar, and Republic of South Africa.
Astrological associations: Taurus and Libra.
Chakra: Heart.
Lifestyle qualities: Rose quartz is like a bubble bath for the emotions. It promotes beauty, both internal and external, and will boost love on all levels, from self-love, which will help you feel better about yourself, to friendship, romance, relationships, and marriage. Rose quartz washes away unhealthy emotions like stress and tension, fear and phobias, anger, guilt, grief, inadequacy, jealousy, and resentment. It will allow you to recover from hurtful childhood memories and emotional wounds, and eases upset, quarrels, and tense situations. Rose quartz inspires creativity, art, music, writing, and imagination and is good in a crisis, bringing forgiveness and calming, feminine energy to any situation.

PINK BANDED AGATE

A variety of agate, this crystal shows pink, white, and possibly gray banding and patterns.

Common source: Botswana.

Astrological associations: Scorpio and Taurus.

Chakra: Heart and Sacral.

Lifestyle qualities: This special crystal brings a soft, loving energy that will help you to connect with your feminine side. It offers universal love and promotes feminine strength, nurturing, and faithfulness. This crystal will help to alleviate depression and stress. Pink banded agate promotes creativity and attention to detail, helping you to see the whole picture and find solutions to problems.

RHODOCHROSITE

Rhodochrosite forms masses, druses, botryoidal structures, and more rarely small, rhombohedral crystals. It can range in color from pale pink to deep red, yellow, orange, and brown. The massive material commonly displays pink and white banding when tumble polished.

Common source: Argentina.

Astrological associations: Scorpio and Leo.

Chakra: Heart.

Lifestyle qualities: Rhodochrosite brings passion to everything you do, promoting sexual energy and generally helping life to flow. It promotes memory and courage, balancing your female and male energies, and easing the symptoms of nervous breakdown and emotional trauma. Combined with rhodonite (see right), it will alleviate 21st-century stress. Improves musicality.

RHODONITE

This stone forms tabular crystals and masses, usually with veined inclusions of manganese that show as black lines through the structure. Color ranges from pale pink to deep red, yellow, orange, and brown.

Common source: Australia, Madagascar, Republic of South Africa, UK (Cornwall), and USA.

Astrological associations: Taurus.

Chakra: Heart.

Lifestyle qualities: Connected to music and artistry, rhodonite promotes sensitivity and attention to detail. It transforms disturbing sounds into music for the mind, alleviating anxiety, mental unrest, confusion, and inconsistency. Combined with rhodochrosite (see left), this calming stone balances your female and male energy, and will alleviate 21st-century stress. Rhodonite boosts self-esteem and memory. It's grounding energy roots love in the real world, helping you choose the right partner and bringing unconditional spiritual love.

KUNZITE

Kunzite is the pink variety of spodumene. It forms flattened, vertically striated, prismatic crystals. Other colors can include lilac, blue, green (hiddenite), yellow and clear (spodumene), and sometimes bi- or tri-colored crystals.

Common source: Afghanistan, Brazil, Madagascar, and Pakistan.

Astrological associations: Scorpio, Taurus, Libra, Aries, and Leo.

Chakra: Heart.

Lifestyle qualities: This crystal promotes love, relationships, and marriage, and can help you to discover your sexuality. Kunzite brings desire to the surface and so can also help with addiction, allowing you to review and consider whether you really want particular substances or behaviors, or not. It is a good crystal for letting go —it will help you release unhelpful behavior patterns, deep-seated feelings, and the need to control everything. Helpful for alleviating depression, stress-related conditions, and energy blocks that cause physical disease. It also disperses negativity in the environment and so will ease the atmosphere after arguments. This calming, centering crystal allows life to flow better, protecting your energy, boosting self-esteem and expression, aiding meditation, and making you feel better overall.

PINK OPAL

This pink stone is a type of common opal without fire (iridescence), which forms in masses.

Common source: Peru.

Astrological associations: Cancer.

Chakra: Heart.

Lifestyle qualities: Pink opal is connected with love, relationships, marriage, rebirth, and renewal. It will change unhelpful behavior patterns, particularly violent behavior. Pink opal clears the mind, allowing inner space to think. This helps with self-healing, and with starting and maintaining the meditative state that will eventually lead to spiritual awakening.

STRAWBERRY QUARTZ

With a color just like mushed strawberries, this crystal forms as massive quartz rock.

Common source: Republic of South Africa.

Astrological associations: Libra.

Chakra: Heart and Crown.

Lifestyle qualities: Strawberry quartz helps you to see the reality in any situation and channels away energy you are not using, leading to peace of mind, calmness, and restful sleep. It brings love.

Multicolor and rainbow

Rainbow crystals attract variety and originality into your life. Multicolored crystals bring a multitude of benefits.

LABRADORITE

Masses of plagioclase feldspar with albite, occasionally forming tabular crystals. It may be gray-green, pale green, blue, colorless, or gray-white in color. The brilliant flashes of blue, red, gold, and green are due to light interference within the structure of the mineral's composition.

Common source: Canada, Madagascar, and Norway.

Astrological associations: Sagittarius, Scorpio, and Leo.

Chakra: Crown.

Lifestyle qualities: Labradorite helps to free your mind, allowing energy to flow around you, magic to happen, and your dreams to manifest. It will help you to see science and magic at the same time. This stone brings mental balance and sharpness. It will boost your aura, relieving anxiety and stress and creating a feeling of confidence that inspires security, originality, and ambition.

FIRE AGATE

This crystal is a variety of agate that occurs as pebbles in brownish colors. Its flashes of "fire" (iridescent colors) are due to thin layers of limonite.

Common source: Mexico.

Astrological associations: Aries.

Chakra: Brow.

Lifestyle qualities: Fire agate promotes inspiration and action, freeing your mind from the shackles of convention, preventing burnout, and helping you to reenergize. This crystal promotes your connection to spirit, enhancing your personal spirituality and your psychic skills of clairvoyance. It acts as a protective psychic shield that dispels fear and helps you to regain emotional control.

OPAL

Forming masses, opal occurs in a multitude of colors, including pink, black, beige, blue, yellow, brown, orange, red, green, and purple. It sometimes shows "fire" (iridescence) in various colors, caused by the diffraction of light within the crystalline structure. Common opal does not have a diffraction grating in its structure and so shows no color.

Common source: Australia, Ethiopia, Peru, and USA.

Astrological associations: Cancer, Libra, Pisces, and Scorpio.

Chakra: Heart, Throat, and Crown.

Lifestyle qualities: Opal removes inhibition. It releases both positive and negative characteristics, allowing you to build on good qualities and deal with the bad. It boosts creativity, inspiration, imagination, all psychic abilities, shamanic visions, and memory.

CHALCOPYRITE

Chalcopyrite forms as tetrahedral crystals with sphenoid faces, octahedral crystals, and masses known as peacock ore. There are usually several bright, iridescent colors in the same mass, including gold, blue, green, and purple. The color occurs due to natural oxidation of the surface, and while scratching may remove the bright colors leaving a gray rock, it will re-oxidize naturally over time if left alone.

Common source: Brazil and Mexico.

Astrological associations: Capricorn.

Chakra: Crown.

Lifestyle qualities: Chalcopyrite balances the right and left hemispheres of the brain, changing your perception and awareness of the environment around you and allowing you to see opportunities presented to you. It removes energy blocks, helps you to balance rising and falling energy levels, enhances your connection to the Universe, and improves all psychic abilities. This crystal is helpful in any form of meditation, helping you to reach and maintain peak experience.

ABALONE SHELL

The shell of a marine mollusk, abalone shell contains minerals that give it a range of brilliant colors.

Common source: Oceans around most continents, particularly Australia, Japan, Mexico, New Zealand, USA, and Vietnam. In many countries it is illegal to collect wild abalone shell but there are plenty available from farms—please check the source when purchasing.

Astrological associations: Aquarius, Cancer, Scorpio, and Pisces.

Chakra: Throat.

Lifestyle qualities: Abalone shell helps you to see the beauty around you. It encourages connection with ancestors and aids communication with animals. It promotes relaxation, femininity, love, and physical strength. It reduces physical tension, allowing you to release trapped emotions.

RAINBOW FLUORITE

This stone is found in cubic, octahedral, and rhombododecahedral crystals and masses. Several colors may occur in one specimen, including green, purple, blue, and clear or colorless bands.

Common source: China and Mexico.

Astrological associations: Pisces and Capricorn.

Chakra: Brow.

Lifestyle qualities: Rainbow fluorite focuses the mind. It aids meditation, concentration, and decision making and is good for stress, allowing the mind to work effectively in intense situations. It promotes healthy, loving relationships, and will focus any partnership, group, or team on their common goal. It will bring order to chaos, helping to calm over-excitement and resolve disputes. Rainbow fluorite also relieves the tiring effects of excessive screen time, such as depression and insomnia.

TOURMALINE

Forming vertically striated, prismatic crystals in most colors including green verdelite, blue indicolite, pink elbaite, red rubellite, yellow tsilasite, black schorl, brown dravite, green or blue with pink center (watermelon) or colors reversed, lime green often with white center, colorless achroite, lavender, bi-colors, tri-colors, and others.

Common source: Brazil, Pakistan, Republic of South Africa, and USA.

Astrological associations: Libra.

Chakra: All (depending on color).

Lifestyle qualities: This calming crystal will protect both people and possessions and is helpful if you are accident-prone. An excellent crystal to support mental health and healing, it will bring mental balance, ease negative thoughts and troubled minds, and help insomnia. It alleviates fear and worry (particularly worry about what other people think of you) and discourages a victim mentality. Tourmaline can illuminate your career and life path, giving a sense of freedom and exploration. It opens your awareness to opportunities, new beginnings, and possibilities, which will enhance reputation and bring fame. It boosts self-confidence and creativity, and in business, it will aid negotiation skills. Tourmaline helps you to look on the bright side of life and see the funny side of situations. It will enhance your connection to nature and help those with a deep desire to save the planet.

MOONSTONE

Moonstone is a variety of feldspar that exhibits chatoyancy. Its colors include white, cream, yellow, brown, blue, green, black, and rainbow (white with a blue flash).
Common source: India.
Astrological associations: Cancer, Libra, and Scorpio.
Chakra: Sacral.
Lifestyle qualities: Moonstone facilitates change, new beginnings, and endings by boosting your awareness of cycles and repeated patterns in your life. This calming stone promotes the exploration of your inner self, easing your emotions during times of change and helping to remove energetic blocks that are holding you back. It will help you to understand your soul's need to roam and explore—possibly to travel or be creative—and trust in your own intuition and insight. Moonstone dispels oversensitivity and pessimism. It promotes wisdom, composure, peace of mind, a caring attitude, and compassion, and boosts confidence, sexuality, and passion, all of which lead to a happy home. Moonstone also brings luck and will attract helpful people into your life.

ANGEL AURA QUARTZ

Quartz crystal bonded with platinum and silver.
Common source: USA (from Arkansas or Brazilian quartz) and China (lower quality at time of writing).
Astrological associations: All.
Chakra: All.
Lifestyle qualities: Boosting your aura and your connection with angels, spirit guides, and divinity, angel aura quartz speeds karma and access to the Akashic records. This protective stone supports nurture, empathy, love, peace, harmony, and those working in caring professions.

TITANIUM QUARTZ

Quartz crystal bonded with titanium and niobium.
Common source: USA (from Arkansas or Brazilian quartz) and China (lower quality at time of writing).
Astrological associations: All.
Chakra: All (especially Crown).
Lifestyle qualities: Titanium quartz is a feel-good crystal that stimulates energy flow, helping you to find your own true path through life. It will center your emotions when you feel wobbly inside. It will aid career decisions, allowing you to see things from different perspectives and other points of view. Titanium quartz promotes change, supporting you through life's challenges, ebbs, and flows. It aids meditation and can help you see auras.

Blue

Blue crystals are connected to spiritual awakening. They promote serenity and self-expression.

BLUE LACE AGATE

This crystal is a variety of agate with pale, blue-and-white bands.
Common source: Namibia.
Astrological associations: Pisces.
Chakra: Throat.
Lifestyle qualities: This gentle, calming crystal brings balance and emotional stability. It promotes faithfulness in marriage and partnership. It raises spiritual awareness and improves communication on all levels.

BLUE CHALCEDONY

Blue chalcedony is a massive form of quartz with inclusions of copper, which give this crystal its blue color.
Common source: Namibia.
Astrological associations: Cancer and Sagittarius.
Chakra: Throat.
Lifestyle qualities: Blue chalcedony aids communication. It helps you to release and share emotions, and can help ease childhood issues or the effects of childhood trauma in adult life.

AZURITE

Found in azure or paler blues, azurite forms in masses and nodules, and more rarely, in tabular and prismatic crystals.
Common source: China, Morocco, and USA.
Astrological associations: Sagittarius.
Chakra: Throat.
Lifestyle qualities: Azurite enhances individuality and is a great crystal for celebrating your uniqueness. It brings compassion, empathy, and improved psychic abilities, as well as helping with creativity and the expression of feelings.

APATITE

Apatite forms prismatic crystals and masses. Colors include blue, yellow, green, white, purple, brown, or red-brown.

Common source: Brazil, Myanmar, and Mexico.

Astrological associations: Gemini.

Chakra: Throat.

Lifestyle qualities: Apatite clears mental confusion. It strengthens your inner self, so you can start to see the truth, end harmful relationships, and be open to new, healthy ones. It lessens the need for emotional eating and so can help with weight balance (either gain or loss). This crystal balances your female and male energies and promotes intellect. Apatite calms the Throat chakra, which makes it a good crystal for healers, communicators (such as teachers, trainers, journalists, writers, and presenters), and performers (such as actors and singers). It reduces aloofness and negativity, making you more approachable. It also aids meditation and all psychic abilities, especially past-life recall and understanding.

KYANITE

This crystal forms blade-type crystals, fibers, and masses. As well as blue, other colors of kyanite can include black, gray, white, green, yellow, and pink.

Common source: Brazil.

Astrological associations: Taurus, Libra, and Aries.

Chakra: Throat.

Lifestyle qualities:

Kyanite is associated with clear communication, and is a good crystal for expressing your truth, telling it how it is, networking, and improving your singing voice. Kyanite aligns the chakras, balances male and female energies, and can help you get started with meditation, bringing you tranquility and calm. It is good for perseverance, reason, connection with spirit guides, dream recall and understanding, attunements and sacred ceremony, psychic awareness, mental stamina, and energy blocks.

AQUAMARINE

Aquamarine is a blue/green variety of beryl. It forms hexagonal, prismatic crystals with flat or occasionally small, pyramidal terminations.

Common source: Afghanistan, Brazil, Namibia, Pakistan, and USA.

Astrological associations: Gemini, Pisces, and Aries.

Chakra: Throat.

Lifestyle qualities: Aquamarine brings learning, spiritual awareness, and development. It helps you see the truth about yourself and recognize your inner talents and beauty, so you can bring forth your best characteristics and step into your power. This crystal is associated with clear communication, allowing you to express your truth and take responsibility for your own actions. Aquamarine can help life flow, and in stressful times, it can be calming and centering. It promotes courage and compassion, attracting helpful people into your life and protecting you on your travels, especially over water.

ANGELITE

Angelite forms as blue/white nodules, masses, and, occasionally, as crystals.
Common source: Peru.
Astrological associations: Aquarius.
Chakra: Throat.
Lifestyle qualities: Angelite allows you to see problems from all angles, and to communicate the answers on many levels. It is particularly helpful for those who work with numbers and numeracy. Angelite can shift your awareness, helping you to connect to your angels, guardians, totem animals, and other spirit helpers. It promotes feelings of security and gives comfort in grief.

BLUE CALCITE

Blue calcite forms in masses.
Common source: Mexico.
Astrological associations: Cancer.
Chakra: Throat.
Lifestyle qualities: Blue calcite gives emotional security, allowing calm communication. This feel-good crystal supports creativity, study, and connection to spirit, helping all children and anyone who has trouble with holding attention, restlessness, concentration, or impulsive behavior.

CELESTITE

This crystal forms as tabular orthorhombic crystals, nodules, and masses. It is found in shades of blue but also occurs in white, yellow, orange, red, and red-brown colors.
Common source: Madagascar.
Astrological associations: Gemini.
Chakra: Brow and Crown.
Lifestyle qualities: Celestite helps you to make connections from your heart and connects you to dreams you may have lost along your way, your goals, and your desires. It promotes the dream state, and will help with dream recall and finding answers in your dreams, while shielding you from nightmares. Celestite is good for clear thought and helps those expressing complex ideas. It aids speech and creative expression. It is linked with creativity and will boost natural talents such as musical or artistic ability. Celestite promotes all types of relationship and supports respectful love. It offers relaxation, stress relief, and diminishing worries. It is good for meditation, connects you to the divine, and is a crystal linked very strongly to angels.

LAPIS LAZULI

Lapis lazuli forms as massive rock and cubic and dodecahedral crystals. The rock almost always includes lazurite, calcite, and pyrite.

Common source: Afghanistan and Chile.

Astrological associations: Sagittarius.

Chakra: Brow.

Lifestyle qualities: Lapis lazuli is connected to knowledge, self-cultivation, and creative expression. It enhances all psychic and natural abilities, and improves mental endurance, organizational skills, and focused communication. It is also a relaxing crystal that aids sleep, relieves insomnia, encourages the dream state, and helps with dream recall and finding answers in your dreams. Lapis lazuli is a happy stone that dispels loneliness and depression. It balances your female and male energies leading to healthy, loving relationships.

AQUA AURA

Aqua aura is quartz crystal bonded with gold, creating beautiful, mostly transparent or translucent blue crystals and clusters.

Common source: USA (from Arkansas or Brazilian quartz) and China (lower quality at time of writing).

Astrological associations: Leo.

Chakra: Throat and Brow.

Lifestyle qualities: Aqua aura boosts the aura, soothing trauma and offering protection. It enhances your connection to divine energy and improves psychic abilities and communication. It's a crystal that just makes you feel better, alleviating negativity, depression, sadness, loss, and grief.

SAPPHIRE

Sapphire is the gem variety of corundum. It is found in any color, except red (which is ruby), including blue, yellow, green, black, violet, pink, and white.

Common source: India, Madagascar, Sri Lanka, and Thailand.

Astrological associations: Virgo, Libra, and Sagittarius.

Chakra: Brow.

Lifestyle qualities: Sapphire is connected to dreams and goals, fulfillment of ambition, and manifestation. It promotes spiritual connections so your spirit guides can help you see the beauty in everything. Sapphire brings fun, joy, and happiness into your life, reducing depression and burnout, and promoting the emotional balance and wisdom that will help you to control compulsions and compulsive behavior.

SODALITE

This crystal forms masses, nodules, and rare dodecahedral and hexagonal prismatic crystals. Occurring in blue, or blue and white, other colors of sodalite include gray, green, yellow, white, red, and colorless.

Common source: Brazil.

Astrological associations: Sagittarius.

Chakra: Brow.

Lifestyle qualities: Sodalite is good for endurance, helping you to focus on objectives and ignore distractions. It will bring teams and groups onto the same wavelength, boosts creativity, and helps to promote ideas and communicate feelings. It is a calming crystal, supporting self-esteem and dispelling fear, insomnia, mental unrest, oversensitivity, confusion, and feelings of inadequacy.

TURQUOISE

This blue, green, or blue-green stone forms as masses, crusts, and rare, small, short prismatic crystals.

Common source: China, Mexico, Myanmar, Tibet, and USA.

Astrological associations: Sagittarius, Pisces, and Scorpio.

Chakra: Throat.

Lifestyle qualities: Turquoise brings the mental and spiritual clarity to see your own path so you can "walk your walk." It improves confidence and courage, clarity, public speaking, and writing, helping you to express your truth, be open to communication, and attract helpful people into your life. It enhances compassion, dispels suspicion and negativity, and rekindles old relationships, friendships, and loves. This lucky crystal helps you to see the beauty in everything and is good for traveling, protecting you on your journey through life and from misfortune (especially natural events or those related to property). It will bring peace of mind and is good for meditation, balancing female and male energy, grounding peak experiences, and promoting wisdom, spirituality, and psychic abilities.

Violet

Energizing violet crystals boost spiritual awareness and change your perception of your world.

SPIRIT QUARTZ

A variety of amethyst or quartz crystal with multiple small crystals growing in a perpendicular cluster all around the main crystal, sometimes with orange/brown iron inclusions or surface staining.
Common source: Republic of South Africa.
Astrological associations: Pisces, Virgo, Aquarius, and Capricorn.
Chakra: Crown.
Lifestyle qualities: This collaborative crystal eases social pressure and aids patience and communication, making it helpful for families, partnerships, teams, group projects, or any situation where there are several people or companies involved in a venture or sport. Spirit quartz gives a sense of belonging, and is good for loneliness and grief. Protective spirit quartz releases and revitalizes emotions and promotes self-esteem and abundance, helping you to learn new lessons and move your life forward. It promotes dreams and can help you to connect to spirit and to your higher self, remember past experiences through meditation, explore your dark side, and challenge your own fear of success.

PURPLE FLUORITE

Purple fluorite crystals appear to grow as steps or citadels, which are often white or clear underneath deep purple. This crystal can also occur as purple or purple-clear, cubic, octahedral, and rhombododecahedral crystals and masses.
Common source: Worldwide (especially China, Mexico, UK, and USA).
Astrological associations: Pisces and Capricorn.
Chakra: Crown.
Lifestyle qualities: Purple fluorite promotes learning and knowledge. It improves focus and cognitive ability, bringing order out of chaos and helping you to work things out, especially when you are stressed. It can also help with screen fatigue. It promotes communication and healthy, loving relationships.

SUGILITE

Suglite forms in masses and rare, tiny crystals.
Common source: Republic of South Africa.
Astrological associations: Virgo.
Chakra: Crown.
Lifestyle qualities: Sugilite is connected to children and is good for child development, especially indigo and crystal children (see Glossary, page 138) and those considered to be neurodivergent, such as those on the autism or dyslexia spectrum. It is good for mental health, boosts creativity, and gives confidence and courage. It fosters spiritual love, offering forgiveness and dispelling hostility, anger, jealousy, prejudice, and despair. The perfect crystal for those embracing difference, sugilite helps you to be who you are and follow your true, life path.

AMETHYST

Amethyst is the violet variety of quartz found as crystals or masses. Its classic purple color is due to manganese and iron inclusions. Other forms of amethyst include the rare, almost black amethyst, the purple-and-white banded amethyst, and green amethyst, which is colored by mineral inclusions.

Common source: Worldwide (especially Brazil, India, Madagascar, Republic of South Africa, and Uruguay).

Astrological associations: Pisces, Virgo, Aquarius, and Capricorn.

Chakra: Crown.

Lifestyle qualities: Amethyst helps your soul tell your spirit what's good for it, allowing you to move forward in life. It helps life flow, easing changes and promoting wise choices. This spiritual crystal can bring purification into ceremonies and is good for meditation, reiki, and the aura. It will enhance your connection to the divine, bringing spirituality into your business, career, and lifestyle, and leading to success in any venture. It aids public speaking, negotiation skills, and self-esteem and boosts cooperation, trust, clarity, confidence, fame, and reputation. Amethyst brings physical and mental balance. It can help with infections which might stop you from performing at your best and also provides emotional energy that will ease grief, homesickness, insomnia, and oversensitivity. It is a calming, peaceful, relaxing crystal that can help you cope with responsibility or stresses that trigger the fight-or-flight response, and so can help to overcome negative coping mechanisms (such as addition, OCD, anger, or violent tendencies). This protective crystal eases insomnia and guards against nightmares, while promoting nighttime dreams and dream recall. Amethyst also magnifies the energy of other crystals.

BANDED AMETHYST

Forming crystals and masses with purple amethyst and white snow quartz, banded amethyst forges a chevron pattern, possibly with rusty red/orange/yellow colors. Zebra amethyst (found in Zambia) has extreme, distinct banding.

Common source: India, Russia, and the Republic of Zambia.

Astrological associations: All.

Chakra: Brow and Crown.

Lifestyle qualities: Banded amethyst is good for longer-term aims. It is good for pain relief, helping with problem solving by taking pain away from difficult decisions and easing chronic pain, which can be debilitating.

AMETRINE

Ametrine is mixture of amethyst and citrine. It is purple and gold in color.

Common source: Bolivia.

Astrological associations: Libra.

Chakra: Solar Plexus and Crown.

Lifestyle qualities: Ametrine frees your mind and promotes an intellectual understanding of spirituality. This crystal dispels prejudice, ignorance, and stubbornness and boosts inspiration and creative thought. It can help you to see any changes you need to make, balance the female and male energies inside you, and bring wealth and prosperity. Ametrine is marvelous for meditation, moving you to your deepest (or highest!) state, bringing peacefulness and a sense of tranquility.

CHAROITE

Forming masses, sometimes with inclusions of white quartz and black manganese.

Common source: Russia.

Astrological associations: Sagittarius and Scorpio.

Chakra: Crown.

Lifestyle qualities: Charoite brings your spiritual experiences into your physical world. It promotes meditation and intuition, helping you be in the moment and see opportunities so you can move forward. It helps life flow, letting go of old relationships, breaking lifestyle cycles and repeated patterns. It is generally good for your mental health and can assist those with neurodiversity, such as those on the autism or dyslexia spectrum. It is also good for any analytical career.

SUPER SEVEN

This type of included quartz, which occurs primarily in a purple color, is comprised of seven different minerals: amethyst, cacoxenite, goethite, lepidocrocite, quartz, rutile, and smoky quartz. Due to these minerals, it may have areas that look brown, red, white, black, and colorless. Smaller pieces exhibit all the healing qualities, even though all seven minerals may not be present in the specimen—the original mass gives super seven it's wonderful healing potential.

Common source: Only one location—Espirito Santo, Brazil.

Astrological associations: All.

Chakra: All.

Lifestyle qualities: Associated with karma, reincarnation, and past lives, super seven offers peace, harmony, love, and spiritual connection. Promoting truth and creativity, this crystal is good for the advancement and fulfillment of dreams, goals, and ideals, and for Earth healing.

LEPIDOLITE

Formed as masses, layered "plates" ("books"), and short prismatic and tabular crystals. Lepidolite occurs in a variety of colors, including lavender (pink to purple), yellow, gray, colorless, and white.

Common source: Brazil.

Astrological associations: Libra.

Chakra: Heart and Brow.

Lifestyle qualities: Lepidolite aids transition. Although it can help with the transition between life and death, it is not limited to this. This awareness-boosting crystal will help you to recognize the things you need to leave behind and to start to make changes. Focused on breaking cycles and unhelpful patterns (such as addictions), lepidolite will help you to learn from experience, calm your energy, and feel good. It aids all stress-related conditions, including depression and lethargy.

White and clear

White and clear crystals stimulate insight and positive energy, helping your life to flow better.

QUARTZ CRYSTAL

Forming hexagonal crystals and masses, quartz is clear or white, sometimes with inclusions.

Common source: Worldwide, including USA (Arkansas), Brazil, China, Madagascar, Russia, Republic of South Africa, and Tibet.

Astrological associations: All.

Chakra: All.

Lifestyle qualities: The all-singing, all-dancing crystal that brings a zest for life, quartz is associated with living life to the full and improving quality of life. It wards away negativity and is good for health conditions on all levels, from physical and mental to emotional and spiritual. Quartz helps you to focus, meditate, and connect to spirit.

APOPHYLLITE

Apophyllite occurs as cubic and pyramidal crystals, druses, and masses. It is commonly white or colorless, although there is a rarer, green variety.

Common source: India.

Astrological associations: Libra and Gemini.

Chakra: Brow and Crown.

Lifestyle qualities: Apophyllite can act as a mirror for inner reflection, promoting truth in all you do. It enhances connection to spirit, will boost brain power, and help to keep you in the present moment.

LEMURIAN QUARTZ CRYSTAL

Lemurian quartz forms clear, quartz, hexagonal crystals with small terminations and horizontal "barcode" striations on its sides. According to legend, when Lemurian priests foresaw that their civilization was about to end in catastrophe, they programmed these crystals with the knowledge and wisdom of their society, sealing them in caves until the time was right for rediscovery.

Common source: Brazil, Colombia, and Russia.

Astrological associations: All.

Chakra: All.

Lifestyle qualities: Lemurian crystal will help you to connect to the divine, to spirit, and to ancestors. It gives a zest for life, allowing you to live life to the full. It's good for big life changes, bringing the wisdom and knowledge of how to cope in troubling times. Lemurian crystal will be a friend when you need one, opening the heart, dispelling negativity, and improving quality of life, making you feel happier. It aids focus and will bring focus to your meditations.

DALMATIAN STONE

Like its namesake, the dalmatian dog, this crystal is white with black dots. It is a mixture of quartz, microcline, and arfvedsonite.

Common source: Mexico.

Astrological associations: Gemini.

Chakra: Base.

Lifestyle qualities: A calming stone that's good for children, education, and creativity, dalmatian stone connects physical and spiritual energy, helping you to achieve your goals. It will balance your female and male energies, promoting healthy, loving relationships full of devotion, fulfillment, and happiness. It helps you let go of the past and release any negativity you may be holding on to.

DANBURITE

Danburite forms prismatic, striated crystals that are colored clear or white, pink, yellow, and lilac.

Common source: Mexico and USA.

Astrological associations: Leo.

Chakra: Crown.

Lifestyle qualities: This crystal boosts socialization and can help with getting back into the world after an absence for any reason, such as breakdown, illness, addiction, or incarceration. It also helps with post-operative depression.

HERKIMER DIAMOND

Herkimer diamond is a clear, stubby, double-terminated quartz crystal.

Common source: Only one location—Herkimer County, New York, USA.

Astrological associations: Sagittarius.

Chakra: Crown.

Lifestyle qualities: This crystal helps you be in the moment. It promotes spontaneity, dispels fear and stress, and makes new beginnings much easier. It is renowned for its ability to attune you to new energies, such as people, places, and deities, to ceremonies and experiences, such as reiki. It mobilizes memory and enhances relaxation.

MAGNESITE

Magnesite forms masses and nodules (which look a bit like 200-million-year-old chewing gum!) More rarely, magnesite can form rhombohedral, prismatic, tabular, and scalenohedral crystals. It is usually white, but also gray, brown, and yellow. It is sometimes dyed and used to imitate more expensive stones.
Common source: Worldwide (especially Republic of South Africa).
Astrological associations: Aries.
Chakra: Crown.
Lifestyle qualities: Magnesite promotes meditation and visualization. It grounds your intellect and boosts passion and love.

HOWLITE

Howlite forms nodules, masses, and rare crystals. It is often dyed and used to imitate more expensive stones.
Common source: USA.
Astrological associations: Gemini.
Chakra: Crown.
Lifestyle qualities: Howlite can boost the immune system, so it is a helpful crystal if you are meeting lots of different people or going into a different environment, such as a new job or traveling. It promotes calm communication and helps both teaching and learning. Howlite gives a sense of fulfillment.

SELENITE

Selenite is a crystallized form of gypsum, sometimes known as satin spa. It is usually clear or white.
Common source: Mexico, Morocco, and USA.
Astrological associations: Taurus.
Chakra: Crown.
Lifestyle qualities: Named after the lunar goddess, Selene, this crystal is linked with the Moon and can help to ease cycles (especially those linked to lunar cycles). It is a cleansing crystal, which can help to release past trauma, freeing you to fulfill your fullest potential. Selenite offers a youthful outlook, boosts passion and sex drive, and promotes longevity.
CAUTION: Not suitable as an elixir.

SNOW QUARTZ

Massive form of quartz.
Common source: Worldwide (especially USA and India).
Astrological associations: Capricorn.
Chakra: Crown.
Lifestyle qualities: Snow quartz clears mental blockages and negative thoughts, creating a space in the mind for creativity, new information, ideas, and clarity of thought. It's good for study and exam revision. Brings longevity, purity, and wisdom to children.

TOURMALINATED QUARTZ

Tourmalinated quartz is a variety of quartz with black, tourmaline crystal rods growing through it.
Common source: Brazil.
Astrological associations: All.
Chakra: All.
Lifestyle qualities: Tourmalinated quartz will help you to see all possible paths that lie ahead and all angles of a situation at once. It is good for problem solving because it promotes lateral thinking. It is also helpful for exploring childhood experiences and related behavior patterns, dispelling depression, fear, and nervous exhaustion.

Black

Black crystals help you see your inner hidden self.

LARVAKITE

Larvakite is a black form of feldspar, sometimes with sheen or iridescent flashes of color.

Common source: Norway.

Astrological associations: Sagittarius, Scorpio, and Leo.

Chakra: Base, Throat, Brow, and Crown.

Lifestyle qualities: Larvakite is associated with the ancient brain (see Fight or Flight, page 89). It can bring emotions to the surface like a volcano erupting, and then soothes the heart, resulting in deep healing. It is grounding and helps you integrate your past with present experience. Larvakite promotes deep thought. This relaxing crystal also promotes sleep, enhancing dreams, and aids understanding and insight from your dreams. It eases insecurity and apprehension.

JET

Jet is the fossilized remains of trees.

Common source: UK and Canada.

Astrological associations: Capricorn.

Chakra: Base.

Lifestyle qualities: Jet can guide you on your life path. It is grounding, brings energy, and offers stamina for long-term projects. It is good for your career and a wealth magnet. Jet offers protection, relieving fear and depression. A calming stone, jet balances female and male energies and promotes sexual energy.

OBSIDIAN

Obsidian occurs as massive volcanic glass. It may be black, brown, green, red-black, brown-black, black with rainbow patterns, black with a silver or gold sheen, or black with snowflake patterns, blue, and purple. It forms translucent black and brown nodules.

Common source: Mexico and US.

Astrological associations: Aries, Sagittarius, Scorpio, and Capricorn.

Chakra: Base.

Lifestyle qualities: Obsidian is the mirror of the soul. It offers you a deep look at yourself, allowing you to see both light and dark sides … and then smile. This grounding crystal connects you to your roots, ancestors, and past experiences. Obsidian will integrate spirituality into your everyday life and career, removing subconscious blockages and self-defeating patterns, and illuminating your life path with all its myriad of possibilities. It is a male stone that brings forth masculine qualities. It also offers protection, aids creativity, learning, and wisdom, and will enhance your ability to cope with grief.

MELANITE

Melanite forms as black, dodecahedral and trapezohedral crystals.

Common source: Brazil and USA.
Astrological associations: Scorpio.
Chakra: Heart.
Lifestyle qualities: Melanite dispels negative emotions, such as jealousy, envy, distrust, anger, resentment, and animosity. It is helpful for the big life changes, such as moving home or divorce.

MERLINITE

Merlinite is a black-and-white, opalized agate with dendritic inclusions of manganese or psilomelane.

Common source: India, Turkey, and USA.
Astrological associations: Pisces.
Chakra: Brow.
Lifestyle qualities: *Carpe diem*— seize the day! Merlinite wants you to seize the moment. This magical stone brings optimism and helps you to move forward in life. It boosts your survival instincts but keeps you calm and will allow you to see both sides of an argument as though the information just appeared in your mind. It helps to balance your female and male energies and sexuality.

TEKTITE

Tektite is meteoritic glass created from the immense heat of a meteorite impact with the Earth. The heat is so intense that both the meteorite and the Earth's surface are melted, and as this mixture of space material and the Earth cool together, tektite is formed. It occurs in black, brown, yellow, and green colors.

Common source: China, Thailand, Indonesia, Libya, and Czech Republic.
Astrological associations: Aries and Cancer.
Chakra: Crown.
Lifestyle qualities: Tektite offers fresh perspectives. It helps you to connect to distant places or other dimensions, enhancing creativity and inspiration. It helps you understand things in different ways, see opportunities and abundance in unexpected places, change how you reason, and open more doors. It helps you explore female and male energies. It aids meditation, from initial focus to peak experience.

Silver and gray

Silver crystals give every cloud a silver lining.

PYRITE

Pyrite forms cubic and dodecahedral crystals and masses, and where it occasionally occurs in flattened form, is known as "pyrite suns." Pyrite may replace many minerals, so can be found in many other formations and in combination with other minerals. Pyrite becomes more golden with oxidation.
Common source: Peru, Spain, USA, and UK.
Astrological associations: Leo.
Chakra: All (especially Solar Plexus).
Lifestyle qualities: This fiery crystal shoots sparks of energy and inspiration. It enhances the mind, memory, thought processes, and leadership abilities and so is good for your career and life path. It wards off negativity and prevents accidents. Pyrite has the magical effect of silencing noisy neighbors or other external disturbances.

GRAY BANDED AGATE

Gray banded agate is a massive variety of chalcedony, displaying gray-and-white bands or patterns.
Common source: Botswana.
Astrological associations: Scorpio.
Chakra: Sacral.
Lifestyle qualities: This crystal stores and releases useable energy, preventing fatigue. It promotes faithfulness in any form of partnership, such as marriage or business.

HEMATITE

Hematite occurs as masses, botryoidal forms, rosettes, layered "plates," tabular, and rhombohedral crystals. It is black and brick-red or brown, taking on a metallic, gray-silver color when polished.

Common source: Worldwide (especially Australia, Brazil, Canada, China, Morocco, Republic of South Africa, UK, USA, and Venezuela).

Astrological associations: Aries and Aquarius.

Chakra: Base.

Lifestyle qualities: One of the best grounding crystals, hematite encourages courage and strength. It enhances dexterity and aids mental processes, memory, meditation, and manifestation (bringing the things we discover through these mental processes into reality). It is helpful for those looking at things from different angles or who work with math or numeracy. Hematite promotes personal magnetism and can help you find a new partner or new love. Hematite supports health on all levels, especially stress-related conditions. It wards off negativity and can help to prevent jet lag, travel sickness, and insomnia.

STIBNITE

Stibnite forms as columns, blades, needle-like, and prismatic crystals with vertical striations and masses.

Common source: China and Uzbekistan.

Astrological associations: Scorpio and Capricorn.

Chakra: Crown.

Lifestyle qualities: Stibnite is linked to traveling. It will help you to discover your path in life, to see the directions you might take, and to make choices and decisions that will ease your journey. This path-finding crystal is associated with the wolf (the totem animal linked to teacher), learning from the wisdom of ancient teachers and masters, as well as all education. Stibnite assists the teacher to clearly communicate information to the student and the student to absorb information from the teacher. Stibnite boosts attractiveness. It is good for attracting helpful people into your life and finding a new partner. It promotes endurance, loyalty in relationships, and faithfulness in marriage or partnership. It helps money matters and fiscal planning. In meditation it keeps distractions at bay.

CAUTION: Not suitable as an elixir.

Brown

Brown crystals stabilize the emotions. They boost stamina, helping you cope with difficult circumstances and enjoy the good ones.

ARAGONITE

Aragonite forms hexagonal, column-shaped crystals that are often linked, twinned, and interpenetrating to form "sputniks." It can also form fibers, masses, and stalactites. Aragonite also occurs in white, brown, yellow, blue, or green.
Common source: Morocco and Namibia.
Astrological associations: Capricorn.
Chakra: Crown.
Lifestyle qualities: Aragonite stills the mind. It relieves stress and anger and breeds patience, practicality, and reliability. It helps with problem solving, allowing you to see things from multiple viewpoints. Answers suddenly become obvious with aragonite.

SEPTARIAN

Septarian forms as nodules of clay ironstone into which other minerals—such as calcite, jasper, dolomite, aragonite, and occasionally barite—are deposited through small cracks in the structure. Other minerals may also be present.
Common source: Australia, Madagascar, and USA.
Astrological associations: Taurus.
Chakra: Base.
Lifestyle qualities: Septarian triggers confidence and clarity of expression, and so can help with public speaking. It promotes both emotional and physical patience, tolerance, flexibility, and endurance. This crystal also increases awareness of the environment and green issues.

PETRIFIED WOOD

Petrified wood forms from fossilized trees, where organic material has been replaced by one or more minerals. The minerals present are usually agate, chalcedony, and quartz, but many other types can also occur. Colors include brown, wood-like colors or agate, chalcedony, and opal colors.
Common source: Worldwide (especially Madagascar and USA).
Astrological associations: Leo.
Chakra: Base.
Lifestyle qualities: Petrified wood can connect you to your ancestors and also promotes connection to the divine. It helps you leave the past behind and move your life forward. It is a grounding stone that soothes the emotions and relieves physical stress. It promotes longevity.

SMOKY QUARTZ

Smoky quartz is a brown or black variety of quartz colored by natural radiation from the earth. This process can be duplicated in laboratories quite effectively, so a lot of the material on the market is clear quartz which has been irradiated.

Common source: Brazil, Madagascar, and USA

Astrological associations: Capricorn and Sagittarius

Chakra: Base

Lifestyle qualities: Smoky quartz is a grounding crystal that helps relieve grief and loss, release tears and bottled-up emotion, and the letting go of sadness, anger, negativity, depression, and despair. It is protective, reflecting energy back to its source, allowing you to move forward in life. It is good for meditation, calming the mind, and breeding relaxation, and can help with dream interpretation. It promotes male yang energy, intuition, and survival instincts.

CRAZY LACE AGATE

Crazy lace agate is a variety of agate with "crazy" patterns, bands, and wavy lines of cream, red, and brown.

Common source: Mexico.

Astrological associations: Capricorn, Aquarius, and Gemini.

Chakra: Heart.

Lifestyle qualities: The go-to crystal for confidence. Crazy lace agate dispels fear and promotes balance, courage, and self-esteem. It also brings faithfulness in marriage or partnership.

MUSCOVITE

Muscovite is a variety of mica, usually occurring as layered "plates", "flowers", "books", scales and masses, and other crystalline forms. Colors include brown, green, pink, gray, violet, yellow, red, and white.

Common source: Brazil.

Astrological associations: Leo and Aquarius.

Chakra: Heart.

Lifestyle qualities: Muscovite acts as a mirror that reflects your innermost feelings and allows you to release painful emotions or issues from the past. It will help you to listen to your intuition and dispel insecurity, self-doubt, pessimism, anger, and excessive worry. It promotes speed of thought, problem solving, and major life decisions. Muscovite reduces excess nervous energy and aids emotional expression, which helps calm tantrums (especially in children). This crystal can balance sleep patterns, easing insomnia, and aid meditation.

RUTILATED QUARTZ

Rutilated quartz is a form of quartz with silver or golden rutile crystals growing through it. The silver or golden color looks like threads or "angel hair."

Common source: Brazil.

Astrological associations: All.

Chakra: Brow and Crown.

Lifestyle qualities: This calming, balancing crystal promotes vitality, strength, physical activity, and lateral thinking. It is good for mental health and healing, warding off breakdown, negativity, and depression.

Further Reading

Bach, Richard, *Illusions: The Adventures of a Reluctant Messiah* (Arrow, 1998)

Berger, Lee, and Hawkes, John, *Cave of Bones* (Disney Publishing Worldwide, 2023)

Dahl, Roald, *The Minpins* (Jonathan Cape, 1991)

Permutt, Philip, *The Modern Guide to Crystal Chakra Healing: Energy medicine for mind, body, and spirit* (CICO Books, 2022)

Permutt, Philip, *Crystal Connections: Understand the messages of 101 essential crystals and how to connect with their wisdom* (CICO Books, 2023)

Permutt, Philip, *The Crystal Healer: Crystal prescriptions that will change your life forever* (CICO Books, 2007)

Wilkins, Dr Jayne et al, *Innovative Homo sapiens behaviours 105,000 years ago in a wetter Kalahari* (NIH: National Library of Medicine, April 2021)

Resources

Ephemeris
https://horoscopes.astro-seek.com/astrology-ephemeris-planetary-online-ephemerides

Philip Permutt's website, with an online crystal shop and details of his workshops, classes, and courses, is found at www.thecrystalhealer.co.uk.

You can also follow him on Facebook (facebook.com/TheCrystalHealer), Twitter (@CrystalHealer), and Instagram (@thecrystalhealer).

Glossary

Acicular Needle-shaped.

ADHD Attention deficit hyperactivity disorder.

Adularescence The appearance of a milky glow from below the surface of the crystal, caused by light diffraction between layers of the mineral. Also known as a schiller effect.

Aggregate A mixture of minerals combined in a geological process; resembles a solid rock.

Akashic records A library of spiritual information that exists on another plane.

Alluvial Made from sediment in riverbeds, which produces "river-tumbled" crystals.

Asterism An optical effect that results in a star-like appearance.

Astral projection The ability to consciously send a part of the astral/spirit body outside the physical body to a specific location (while remaining connected to the physical body).

Astral travel The ability to send a part of the astral/spirit body to travel outside the physical body (while remaining connected to the physical body).

Aura The subtle energy field around the body.

Bladed A crystal that resembles a flat knife blade.

Bodymind The body's energy system, which links mind, body, and spirit.

Botryoidal Describes bulbous minerals that resemble a bunch of grapes.

Brecciated Describes rocks formed from clastic (rock formed from broken pieces of older rock), angular fragments in a matrix of smaller stones and mineral cement.

Chakra The Sanskrit word for "wheel." Chakras are the energy centers of the body, appearing as wheels to people who see energy.

Channeling The communication of messages or information from the spirit world via a medium.

Chatoyancy An optical effect, also known as "cat's eye," found in some polished crystals.

Chi In Chinese medicine and philosophy, *chi* is the energy or life force of the Universe, believed to flow round the body and to be present in all living things. Other cultures call *chi* by different names. For example, *ki* (Japan) and *prana* (India).

Clast A fragment of geological debris—a chunk or smaller grain of rock which has broken off another rock due to physical weathering or seismic activity. Clasts often recombine in another concretion material to form a clastic rock.

Columnar Stout parallel clusters with a column-like appearance.

Concretion Hard, compact mineral mass, often spherical.

Crust The top or outer layer. Crystals occurring as crusts are growing on the surface of a rock or mineral. See also *Druse*.

Cryptocrystalline Microscopic crystalline structure.

Crystal children Children with special abilities, often psychic. A further development, or the next stage, from indigo children. See also *Indigo children*.

Crystal system A classification of crystals according to their atomic structure, describing them in terms of their axes (imaginary straight lines through the center, around which they are symmetrically arranged). The systems are hexagonal, isometric, monoclinic, orthorhombic, tetragonal, and triclinic.

Cubic Describes a cube-shaped crystal, with six square faces. The three axes are the same length and are at right angles to one another.

Dendrite A mineral that crystallizes in the shape of a tree or branch or grows through another crystal of rock, creating the impression of a tree or branches.

Dodecahedral Describes a crystal with 12 pentagonal (five-sided) faces meeting in threes at 20 vertexes.

Druse A surface crust of small crystals on a rock of the same or a different mineral.

Earth healing Sending/directing healing energy to the planet.

Elixir A crystal elixir is water in which a crystal has been immersed.

EMF Electromagnetic fields.

Energy A supply or source of power: electrical, nuclear, mechanical, or subtle, such as *chi*.

Enhydro Water bubble(s) trapped in air pocket(s) inside a crystal as it was forming. The water and air inside may be hundreds of millions of years old.

Equant Having different diameters approximately equal, so as to be roughly cubic or spherical in shape.

ESP Extra-sensory perception.

Feldspar A group of silicate minerals.

Fibrous/fiber A rock made up of roughly parallel fine threads.

Fire A play of color caused by dispersion of light within a crystal, such as that shown by diamonds. Fire opal does not necessarily exhibit fire, but occurs in colors of fire—reds, oranges, yellows. Opal does not display true fire but a play of light caused by the scattering of light by microscopic silica spheres in the opal structure.

Flow The Taoist concept of allowing things to happen naturally.

Geopathic stress Energy that emanates from the Earth and is detrimental to human health. Two sources of this energy may be underground moving water or radiation from mobile phone masts. Geopathic stress is linked with a long list of ailments, ranging from headaches to cancer.

Globular Globe-shaped/spherical.

Granular A mineral composed of grains. May be formed with rounded, semi-rounded, or angular grains or can be massive (see *Mass*).

Hexagonal Describes a crystal system having four axes, of which the three horizontal axes are equal in length and cross at 120° angles, and the vertical axis is a different length and at right angles to the others. A hexagonal crystal has eight faces.

Inclusion A mineral found within the structure of a different mineral.

Indigo children Children with special abilities, often psychic. Most indigo children are now grown adults and are at the forefront of the human consciousness movement. See also *Crystal children*.

Iridescence Colors appearing inside a crystal due to either the diffraction or refraction of light within the crystalline structure.

Isometric Describes a crystal system having three axes that are all equal in length and at right angles to one another.

Karma/karmic process/karmic healing Karma equals action or deed. Also refers to cause and effect and specifically to how the actions of an individual can/will affect his/her future. Karmic healing is about healing karma from past lives or this life so you do not take it with you into the next life.

Lamellar Scaly. An aggregate of scales.

Lemuria According to legend, Lemurian civilization was a highly advanced ancient society that predates Atlantis. Priests of Lemuria are believed to have worked extensively with crystals, especially quartz crystals. In the final days before catastrophic destruction, they programmed quartz crystals with the knowledge of their society, sealing them in caves to protect them until the time was right for rediscovery.

Macrocrystalline/macrocrystalline quartz Having crystals large enough to be seen with an unaided eye. This term is used to contrast cryptocrystalline/microcrystalline, where the crystals are too small to be visible to the naked eye.

Manifestation The bringing of your dreams, desires, or goals into physical reality.

Mass Matter that has no definable crystalline structure. When the term massive is used, it refers to this rather than to the size of the crystal.

Mica Individual member of the mica group of related aluminum silicate minerals that are soft and have perfect basal cleavage (when a mineral has only one cleavage plane), which allows individual members to be "peeled."

Monoclinic Describes a crystal system having three unequal axes, only two of which are at right angles.

Nodule A form of mineral that is massive (see *Mass*) with a rounded outer surface.

OCD Obsessive compulsive disorder.

Octahedral Describes a crystal having eight faces that are all equilateral triangles; resembles two four-sided pyramids joined at the bases.

Opalescence Color effect, typically found in opals, which causes a play of light when moved and viewed from different directions.

Orthorhombic Describes a crystal system having three axes of unequal lengths that cross at right angles.

Oxidation A chemical reaction in which oxygen is added to an element or compound, often producing a rust-like appearance.

Piezoelectric effect The electric current produced by some crystals when they are subjected to mechanical pressure.

Phantom When a crystal, typically quartz, stops growing and another mineral is deposited on the surface of the facets making the termination. Sometime later, possibly millions of years, the quartz starts to grow again, growing faster than the other mineral, covering it and leaving a ghostly shape within the crystal.

Plagioclase A series of feldspars, including labradorite and sunstone.

Plate A crystal that has grown flattened and often thin.

Prismatic Describes a crystal having faces that are similar in size and shape and that run parallel to an axis; the ends are rectilinear and similar in size and shape. For example, a triangular prismatic crystal has two triangular ends joined by three rectangular faces, while a

hexagonal prismatic crystal has two hexagonal ends connected by six rectangular faces.

Pseudo- (before a shape, for example, pseudocubic) Assuming a false shape; the crystal is apparently this shape, but not actually so.

Pseudomorph A mineral that replaces another within the original's crystal structure. As a result, the new mineral has the external shape of the departed one.

Psychic abilities These include intuition or gut feelings, channeling, clairaudience, clairsentience, clairvoyance, sensing energies and auras, seeing auras, interpreting auras, telepathy, extrasensory perception, and increased insight into divination and tarot card readings.

PTSD Post-traumatic stress disorder.

Pyramidal Describes a crystal in which the base is a polygon (i.e. with at least three straight sides) and the other faces are triangles that meet at a point.

Pyroelectric effect The production of electric charges on opposite faces of some crystals caused by a change in temperature.

Record keeper Describes a crystal with raised triangles on the face of the termination.

Reiki A form of hands-on healing that originated in Japan and now has millions of practitioners worldwide. The reiki healing ray is the frequency of Reiki energy as it is transmitted in healing.

Reniform Kidney-shaped.

Rhombic Describes rhomboid crystals, i.e. those with a parallelogram shape (a parallelogram has four equal sides and oblique angles).

Rhombododecahedral Describes crystals that have 12 equal sides with oblique angles.

Rhombohedral Describes crystals having six faces, each of them a rhombus (which has four equal sides, with opposite sides parallel, and no right

angles). A rhombohedron resembles a cube that is skewed to one side.

Scalenohedral Describes crystals having 12 faces, each of them a scalene triangle (which has three unequal sides).

Scaly Describes an aggregate of scales, which are small, flattened, overlapping crystals.

Scrying Looking into a crystal ball (or obsidian mirror) to see images to predict the future, or to view the past or present.

Skeletal Describes crystals with gaps in their structure due to periods of unstable growth.

Sphenoid Wedge-shaped.

Stalactites Mineral formations descending from the roof of caverns, created as mineral-rich water drips down, and facilitating the mineral to deposit over thousands or millions of years.

Striated Describes crystals with parallel grooves or markings along their length.

Tabular Describes crystals that are broad and flat; sometimes shortened to "tabby."

Termination The end of the crystal formed by the facets or faces making up the point. Note that a few varieties of crystal have flat terminations, such as some tourmaline and spodumene crystals.

Tetragonal Describes a crystal system having three axes, of which only the two horizontal ones are equal, and all three axes are at right angles. It resembles a cube that has been stretched vertically.

Tetrahedral Describes crystals that have four faces.

Trapezohedral Describes crystals that have trapezium-shaped face. A trapezium is a quadrilateral with two parallel sides.

Triclinic Describes a crystal system having three axes, none of them equal in length or at right angles.

Index of crystals

A

abalone shell 27, 81, 115
agate 19, 40, 79
  blue lace agate 34, 56, 66, 67, 75, 118
  crazy lace agate 135
  fire agate 77, 88, 114
  gray banded agate 132
  pink banded agate 52, 74, 112
amazonite 52, 70, 85, 107
amber 15, 39, 74, 82, 105
amethyst 19, 21, 27, 31, 32, 34, 36, 38, 39, 47, 56, 57, 63, 66, 67, 73, 74, 75, 76, 82, 83, 85, 91, 93, 124
ametrine 27, 52, 73, 77, 124
angel aura quartz 27, 93, 117
angelite 35, 39, 50, 54, 75, 120
apatite blue 12, 75, 86, 119
apophyllite 126
aqua aura 75, 88, 93, 121
aquamarine 27, 56, 65, 66, 75, 76, 78, 85, 93, 119
aragonite 74, 134
aventurine 38, 52, 53, 74, 85, 87, 107
azurite 52, 77, 118

B

banded amethyst 66, 74, 124
bloodstone 19, 52, 66, 110
blue calcite 27, 38, 56, 75, 120
blue chalcedony 56, 75, 91, 118
blue lace agate 34, 56, 66, 67, 75, 118
bowenite 27, 65, 73, 78, 83, 90, 110
brecciated jasper 101

C

calcite 11, 15, 34, 54, 62, 63, 70, 85
  blue calcite 27, 38, 75, 120
  cobaltoan calcite 71, 111
  golden calcite 106
  green calcite 15, 32, 36, 54, 73, 88, 109
  orange calcite 30, 47, 77, 102
  red calcite 100
carnelian 19, 27, 33, 34, 35, 53, 56, 62, 66, 67, 70, 77, 85, 103
celestite 32, 35, 37, 39, 47, 52, 53, 79, 83, 93, 120
chalcopyrite 87, 115
charoite 54, 76, 79, 91, 125
chert 11
chrysocolla 34, 52, 70, 79, 93, 108
chrysoprase 47, 70, 87, 109
citrine 12, 13, 24, 27, 30, 31, 32, 34, 35, 52, 53, 65, 66, 67, 72, 74, 79, 84, 85, 90, 105
cobaltoan calcite 71, 111
copper 27, 70, 79, 106
crazy lace agate 135

D

dalmatian stone 27, 79, 82, 85, 127
danburite 78, 79, 93, 127
dreams 38

E

emerald 27, 109

F

fire agate 77, 88, 114
flint 32
fluorite 32, 33, 39, 53, 61, 62, 63, 74, 79, 85
  purple fluorite 53, 55, 58, 75, 85, 123
  rainbow fluorite 35, 73, 116
  yellow fluorite 52, 53, 85, 106
fuchsite 39, 109

G

garnet 35, 50, 54, 73, 76, 82, 101
golden calcite 106
golden healer quartz 27, 47, 104
granite 33
gray banded agate 132
green calcite 32, 36, 54, 73, 88, 109

H

halite 39, 102
hematite 27, 34, 35, 38, 39, 50, 52, 53, 54, 79, 133
Herkimer diamond 72, 127
howlite 56, 75, 82, 85, 128

J

jade 19, 27, 38, 73, 74, 80, 82, 91, 108
jasper 19, 70, 82
  brecciated jasper 101
  red jasper 37, 38, 47, 53, 67, 100
jet 27, 34, 84, 130

K

kunzite 27, 54, 57, 73, 76, 83, 91, 113
kyanite 34, 38, 56, 63, 66, 75, 78, 119

L

labradorite 10, 34, 77, 83, 87, 92, 114
lamps 38
lapis lazuli 27, 37, 38, 56, 66, 67, 75, 79, 83, 85, 121
larvakite 130
Lemurian quartz crystal 32, 66, 67, 73, 93, 126
lepidolite 34, 54, 70, 73, 82, 85, 91, 125

M

magnesite 128
malachite 27, 37, 67, 86, 107
melanite 131
merlinite 71, 76, 131
miscovite 136
mookaite 38, 52, 74, 75, 76, 80, 100
moonstone 19, 27, 52, 72, 73, 77, 93, 117
morganite 27, 77, 78, 79, 85, 111
muscovite 39, 74

O

obsidian 19, 27, 34, 52, 85, 90, 130
opal 39, 77, 114
  pink opal 27, 113
orange calcite 30, 47, 77, 102

P

peridot 34, 70, 91, 110
petrified wood 27, 32, 39, 90, 93, 134
pink banded agate 52, 74, 112
pink opal 27, 113
purple fluorite 53, 58, 75, 85, 123
pyrite 11, 27, 30, 31, 32, 33, 34, 35, 36, 39, 53, 60, 77, 81, 85, 91, 132

Q

quartz 19, 21, 27, 33, 40, 58
  angel aura quartz 27, 93, 117
  golden healer quartz 27, 47, 104
  Lemurian quartz crystal 32, 66, 67, 73, 93, 126
  quartz crystal 31, 39, 51, 61, 62, 63, 66, 70, 126
  rose quartz 27, 38, 39, 40, 50, 52, 57, 63, 77, 78, 111
  rutilated quartz 77, 86, 136
  smoky quartz 38, 61, 75, 76, 86, 90, 135
  snow quartz 27, 35, 47, 85, 129
  spirit quartz 12, 38, 53, 76, 85, 123
  strawberry quartz 38, 113
  titanium quartz 27, 73, 117
  tourmalinated quartz 74, 77, 129

R

rainbow fluorite 35, 73, 116
red calcite 100
red jasper 37, 38, 47, 53, 67, 100
rhodochrosite 37, 63, 76, 79, 88, 112
rhodonite 32, 35, 53, 59, 79, 88, 112
rose quartz 19, 27, 38, 39, 40, 50, 52, 63, 77, 78, 111
ruby 27, 37, 38, 52, 72, 73, 74, 82, 85, 87, 101
rutilated quartz 77, 86, 136

S

sapphire 83, 121
selenite 21, 31, 32, 38, 39, 63, 128
septarian 56, 75, 93, 134
smoky quartz 38, 61, 75, 76, 86, 90, 135
snow quartz 27, 35, 47, 85, 129
sodalite 38, 52, 53, 75, 122
spirit quartz 12, 38, 53, 76, 85, 123
stibnite 27, 74, 79, 84, 85, 133
strawberry quartz 38, 113
sugilite 27, 54, 80, 123
sunstone 103
super seven 125

T

tektite 32, 84, 131
tiger's eye 18, 19, 27, 34, 35, 37, 54, 72, 77, 84, 86, 104
titanium quartz 27, 73, 117
tourmalinated quartz 74, 77, 129
tourmaline 15, 27, 30, 31, 32, 34, 36, 37, 39, 48–9, 52, 54, 62, 63, 66, 72, 77, 84, 85, 87, 88, 91, 93, 116
turquoise 27, 56, 62, 65, 66, 75, 77, 78, 79, 91, 93, 122

U

unakite 19, 71, 90, 108

V

vanadinite 27, 39, 82, 102

Y

yellow fluorite 52, 53, 106

Index

A

abundance 82, 84
accidents 91
addiction 91
ambition 83
animals 81
anxiety 15, 37, 54, 88
astrology 18–19
aura 18
awareness exercise 17

B

bagua map 26–9
balance 83
bathrooms 39
bedrooms 37–8
being present 71
birthstones 18–19
body, chakras 42–3
bowels 12, 13
brain and crystals 86–7
breath 21
broken crystals 40
butterfly metaphor 73

C

calmness 63, 73
careers 82
caring for crystals 20–1
caring professions 63
caterpillar metaphor 73
chakra sets 66–7
chakras 42–3
challenges 54, 59, 72
change 73, 78
chi 26, 76
children 80
children's bedrooms 38
choosing crystals
    basic overview 14–15

dowsing 98–9
    feng shui 28–9
    specific occasions 30, 70
cleansing crystals 20–1, 58
clutter 60–1
collaboration 85
combining crystals 12
communication 56, 63, 66, 74
commuting 65
computers 32, 55
confidence 49
conflict 57
cooking 33–4
courage 54, 72
creative space 35
creativity 52, 77
customer services 62

D

decision making 74
desires 83
digestion 12, 13, 34
dining rooms 34
divine energy 93
dowsing 98–9
dreams 37, 83

E

earth, burying crystals 21
emotions 56, 86–91
energy
    cleansing 20–1
    divine energy 93
    feng shui 26–9
    personal 62
    room requirements 24
    workplace 58
entryways 31
equilibrium 86–7

F

factories 59–61
feng shui 26–9
fight-or-flight response 88, 89
flow 76
focus 35, 53, 58, 62
friendship 78
fulfilment 82, 83

G

garden furniture 40
geodes 21
gratitude 71
grief 90

H

hallways 31
healing 86
Himalayan salt lamps 32
history of crystal technology 11
hypnotherapy 79

I

incense 21
individuality 48
infections 56
inspiration 77
ions 32, 55

J

jewelry 48
job satisfaction 47
journeys 65–7, 93

K

kitchens 33–4

L
lamps 32
leadership 85
living rooms 31–2
loss 90
love 79
luck 77

M
magic 10, 92
management skills 84–5
massage 63
meditation 36, 50, 51
mental health 54, 86–91
mishaps 91
moment, being in 71
money 84
mood boosters 30, 70
moonlight 21
motivation 53, 83, 87

N
nature 93
negative ions 32, 55
negotiation 85
new beginnings 72
noise 59
numeracy 35, 50

O
office spaces 35, 52–8
outdoor areas of the home 40
overwhelm 58

P
parties 30, 70
pendulums 98–9
plants 40
positive ions 32, 55
problem solving 54

productivity 53, 62
public speaking 56
purpose, finding 82
pyramids 60

R
reaction to crystals, speed
    of 16–17
reiki 21
relationships 78–81
relaxation 89
repetitive tasks 59
rooms see also specific rooms
    chakras 42–3
    energy and mood 24
    feng shui 26–9
rose quartz 57

S
sales jobs 62, 65
science 10
screens 32, 55
self-care 50
self-love 78
sexual passion 37, 79
ship metaphor 71
sleep 37, 83, 86
sound 20
sources 96
spiritual well-being 92
stamina 86
storage areas 39
strength 86
stress 58, 88–9
studying 82, 85
sunlight 21

T
Taoism 76
teamworking 53, 85
technology 54
televisions 32
thankfulness 71
therapy rooms 36
throat infections 56
tingsha 20
trauma 56, 88
traveling 65–7, 93

W
wakes 30
warehouses 59–61
water 21, 32, 39, 55, 93
wealth 84
weight 12, 13, 86
working
    bringing crystals into the
        workplace 48–9
    careers 82
    from home 52
    management skills 84–5
    office-based 53–8
    traveling 65–7
    using crystals, overview 46
warehouses and factories 59–61
with the public 62–3
work–life balance 50
worry 15, 37, 54, 88

Z
zodiac signs 18–19

Acknowledgments

A fabulously big thank you to my fabulous friend Nicci Roscoe for being an inspiration as well as for all your help and support.

I would like to also thank my staff at The Crystal Healer Crystal Showroom, affectionately known as the Crystal Healer Helpers, Claire, Becky, and Rachel. Without them, finding the time to write this book would have been complicated. I am truly grateful to all my clients, customers, students, and friends who inspire me to take the next steps on this glittering crystal path and discover more about the wondrous world of the Stone People every day and help to create the wealth of experience I share with you.

Thanks to the people at CICO Books who turn my words into magical books, particularly Carmel Edmonds who helped get this book off the ground and Kristy Richardson for her patience!!! Thank you, Cindy Richards, for having faith in the beginning, all those years ago.

A loving farewell to my friend and fellow author Martin Baum, who I'm sure is up there in the heavens making the gods laugh.

Finally, the people who inspired me to write: my father Cyril, American crystal healer Melody, and Ian, who knows why.

Picture credits